26 Ways To Screw-Up in Business and How Not To

My 50 years in Advertising and Marketing.

26 Ways To Screw-Up in Business and How Not To

WILLIAM F. FAWCETT

iUniverse, Inc.
Bloomington

26 Ways To Screw-Up in Business and How Not To

iUniverse books may be ordered through booksellers or by contacting:

iUniverse
1663 Liberty Drive
Bloomington, IN 47403
www.iuniverse.com
1-800-Authors (1-800-288-4677)

ISBN: 978-1-4620-2713-2 (sc)
ISBN: 978-1-4620-2714-9 (ebk)

Printed in the United States of America

iUniverse rev. date: 08/05/2011

Contents

Introduction

Change is the law of life . . .

With the introduction of the internet, marketing has radically changed. The media has changed. The way sales messages are conveyed has changed. The marketing mix has changed. Social media now rules. Everything has changed!

No, that's not true; everything has not changed. The customer's buying mentality has not changed. They are still as skeptical as they were fifty years ago. Their buying analysis has not changed.

Also, what has not changed are the reasons that cause businesses to fail. Companies that don't own-a-word will probably fail; executives who place probability before profitability will run out of money; companies who don't put their customers first will come in last; companies who don't inculcate the social media into their marketing mix will not survive; executives who impose self-fears will stunt growth; executive personality quirks won't be tolerated. The power of this book lies not only in identifying these business death knells but in providing practical, proven solutions learned over the last 50 years.

This book is not about managing people; it's about managing oneself. The number one determinant of your success is you! You're the quarterback who gets all the glory when you win and all the blame when you lose. What if you could reduce the number of turnovers and interceptions? Wouldn't you want to know what mistakes you must avoid? Of course you would! This *Guide-To-Success* not only identifies what you must avoid; it offers prescriptions for doing it right.

For nearly five decades I have worked with hundreds of entrepreneurs and small business owners and I know for a fact that 95% of business mistakes are a result of breaking one or more of the 26 commandments set forth in this *Guide-To-Success*.

Over the years, I have witnessed and taken part in many high-dollar sales presentations and advertising campaigns. It's important to remember what I'm going to be sharing with you doesn't come from an ivory-tower perspective but rather it surfaces from the sales trenches.

Unlike some gurus out there, I don't claim to have invented the internet. I don't have all the answers. I don't believe that my approach is the only way to realize success but I do know that if you break the commandments set forth in this book, you have placed your company in a very precarious position. After fifty years of empirical observations and hands-on marketing, I have distilled my findings into twenty-six business commandments that govern success and failure in the marketplace. If violating any one of the commandments was a punishable offense, a large portion of corporate America would be in jail. So violate them at your own risk!

FAWCETT'S 50-YEAR RESUME

IMPORTER OF WINES AND CORDIALS:
Drambuie, Couvoisier Cognac, Tia Maria and Jim Beam Imports

AD AGENCY OWNER—CREATIVE DIRECTOR
Fawcett Advertising, an award-winning agency, purchased by B&J

PRODUCER OF AN OFF-BROADWAY PLAY
Wrote and produced "Breaking-Free" live on-stage: Jane Fonda, Dr. Laura

DOCUMENTARY FILM PRODUCER
"Shotgun Sunday" received a Cannes Film Festival Nomination

TELEVISION PRODUCER-DIRECTOR
Produced and Directed "Athletes-In-Action" TV Series

DIRECT-RESPONSE MAVEN
Produces TV Commercials and Infomercials

INVENTOR US PATENT 3,940,130
A Bull-Fighting Amusement Park Attraction

THAT'S NO BULL!!!

Who's Bill Fawcett? How can he help me grow my business?

Wondering who I am is a valid question. I have spent my entire career of over fifty years making entrepreneurial ventures successful and helping small business owners to get to the next stage. As you can see by my resume, I have had a rich, diverse career. It's only fair, and quite important, that you are comfortable with my credentials and expertise. What better way is there to acquaint you with my background than to tell you a bit about myself and how I've been able to sell millions of dollars of products and services for an international clientele.

Let's start at the beginning. I was born in a quaint, New England seafaring town. From my window I could see waves crashing on the rocks and spraying chilly salt air. We lived three houses down from the lighthouse. It was so cold and chilly, I thought underwear came damp.

My mother was a showgirl and my dad was an art director. My mother didn't marry until she was thirty-three. Back in those days, that was unheard of. To make matters even more risqué, she married a young man of thirty-one years. My mother was the first cougar.

Because my parents had only high-school educations, a great emphasis was placed on this kid being well-educated. I attended the Harvard Business School, Loyola Law School and Boston College. During those golden school days, I had an epiphany. Although I loved Law School, one day the professor snarled: "Mr. Fawcett, your sense of humor is disruptive. If you don't change, I'm fearful that you'll be getting clients with parking tickets the electric chair." I wish I could tell you I changed. I didn't.

To me, intellectual humor is one of the best ways to persuade a person to buy your product or service. To that end, I chose "*The Alacrity of a Joke*" as the subject of my MBA thesis. I remember that day of long ago when I walked down the hallowed halls and into the dean's office. With a broad smile I told him that my thesis was going to be analyzing the speed at which a joke travels and the reasons why. You have to realize this was way back, pre-historic internet. He slowly lowered his glasses to the bridge of his nose and, in a haughty ivory-tower tone, said "Mr. Fawcett, you must be joking." No, I wasn't. The extrapolation of those octane reasons that drive the speed of a joke have been instrumental in me selling millions of dollars of products and services.

Over the years, I have helped more than three hundred start-up companies and mid-size firms get to the next level. During those five decades, I discovered that the reasons for failure were immutable. The mission of this book is to save you from making costly mistakes. I chose to write this book in a fun, memorable "*26 Commandments*" format, so you could recall them in a moment's notice. These Commandments weren't divinely inspired; rather, they were perspired . . . by fifty years of sweat.

Besides consulting and video production, my personal kaleidoscope of entrepreneurial ventures include the writing and producing of *Breaking Free*, a successful off-Broadway motivational show. Major stars like Jane Fonda and Dr. Laura Schlessinger made onstage appearances. Accompanying this book you will find a DVD explaining the communication dynamics learned from the show.

At the height of the tennis explosion (1978), I produced a fun tennis motion picture called *Shotgun Sunday* that was nominated for a Cannes-Film documentary award. On the DVD I will share with you why I produced the *Athletes-in-Action* TV series and what was the secret behind City of Hope's innovative fund-raising program. Today, we continue to produce infomercials and direct-response strategies that will result in selling millions of dollars of products and services.

Now that I'm on the back nine of my life, I want to be a mentor. I want to mentor young business executives, entrepreneurs, small-business owners and especially *old school* marketers who are struggling with how to inculcate *new school* techniques into their marketing mix! That's the reason I wrote this book.

During the course of this pocket business bible, I will share invaluable information that has the power to change your business life. What you choose to do with this new information is up to you. Violate these commandments at your own risk!

1st Commandment:
Thou Shall Own A Word Or Fail

Every major MBA program emphasizes the importance of owning a word. That tidbit of information has just saved you $120,000 in MBA tuition.

To be successful, you need to own a word that makes you number one in a specific category. For example, there were many pizza companies in the market before Domino's Pizza entered into the space. Its founder, Tom Monaghan, knew if he were to be successful he needed to own a word. What was the word Tom chose? Yes, that's right, *home-delivery*. He immediately became number one in home-delivery.

More current is Z Pizza's entrance into the market. Chris Bright, its founder, also knew he needed to own a word phrase to differentiate his pizza from all the others. Words like great, tasty, low-price weren't going to do it. Plus, the pizza category was already jammed with nice adjectives. He made up his own category so he could be number one. To tie-in with America's health kick and green approach, he selected the words *fresh organic ingredients*. He made himself number one in environmental pizzas. Remember, it's better to be first in the prospect's mind than first in the market place. First in the mind is everything. Marketing is a battle of perceptions, not products.

If your product can't be first in a category, set up a new category where you can be first. When you launch a new product or when you're refreshing an old brand, the first question to ask yourself is not how is my product better than the competition but rather, what category can I be number one in? Owning an attribute is probably the number-one way to differentiate a product or service. It's much easier to convince someone you have a better product if you're number one. When you're a leader, people tend to believe almost anything you say. It's called the "halo effect." It's when consumers, of their own volition, attribute other marketing benefits to your product. For example: Prego Spaghetti Sauce owns the word "thicker." The "halo effect" came into play and Prego customers translated the word "thicker" to quality and nourishing ingredients. What I'm proposing is counter-classic marketing thinking, which is brand-oriented. Forget the brand. Think categories. Everyone talks about why their brand is better, but prospects have an open mind when it comes to categories. Customers are on the defensive when it comes to brands. Everyone is interested in what's new. Remember, it's never too late for your company to own a word!

Being first in a category is the first step in wading into the *Blue Oceans*. The term *Blue Oceans* is an analogy that denotes all the industries not in existence today, the unknown market space, untainted by competition,coined by professors Renee Mauborgne and Chan Kim in their book *Blue Oceans Strategy*. In a *Blue Ocean* demand is created rather than fought over. There is ample opportunity for growth that is both profitable and rapid and competition is irrelevant because the rules of the game are waiting to be set.

The premise of the book *Blue Ocean Strategy* is for a company to sustain high performance and profitability. It must look beyond its current environment and create new profit and growth opportunities that are not now in existence. Cirque du Soleil is a great example of creating a *Blue Ocean*, a new market space by blending opera and ballet with the circus format, while eliminating star performers, lions and elephants. They were not just number one in the category; they *were* the category.

In contrast to *Blue Oceans* is the shark-infested *Red Sea*, the known market space where all the industries in existence today are swimming. In the *Red Oceans* industry boundaries are already defined and accepted and the competitive rules of the game are known. Here, companies try to out-perform their rivals to grab a greater share of product or service demand. As the market space gets crowded, prospects for profits and growth are reduced. Products become commodity or niche and cutthroat competition turns the ocean bloody.

Granted that *Blue Oceans* are where you want to be navigating the future, it's portrayed as a business nirvana. The opportunities are without limits.

Sounds good, but it would be wonderful if you could start tomorrow and create a new product for an industry that doesn't exist. That's not going to happen! It's going to take a while, if ever! No matter what, the way you begin the navigation of the *Blue Oceans* is to own your word-phrase as it gets you thinking outside the box. It's like wading into the *Blue Oceans*. It's the starting place.

If you are going to be perceived as the leader in a category, then your word has to have a narrow focus. A good example of that is Federal Express focusing on just one aspect of their business: *Overnight Delivery*. You want to burn your word into the prospects' minds. What is critical for your success is to focus your marketing efforts on perpetuating the perception that you're the best. You're number one. You're the leader in the field with valuable solutions. Once perceived that you're the leader in the category, customers buy off on it. They perceive it to be true. People are seldom, if ever, wrong . . . at least in their own minds.

Ownership words come in three different categories: Benefit, Service and Audience. Let's begin with Benefit. What benefit does your company offer that makes people want to do business with you? Examples: *WebMD Health* offers better information, better health. *Beautyrest* offers a better night's sleep. *Mercedes* offers a better-engineered car. *NutriSystem* offers a healthier life. *Apple Computer* offers two benefits: great graphics and it doesn't crash.

Service-related examples: *Saturn*, which built its brand on no-hassle sales and service for the average American car buyer. *Nordstrom's* offers exceptional CRM services. *Southwest Airlines* is perceived to be the leader in affordable air travel. *Dell* entered the crowded, personal computer field by choosing to be first to sell computers by phone. It doesn't matter how crowded the space is, you can always come-up with a category you can be First in. If you can't, then contact me.

Audience related examples: Define your target market and then search for a word-phase that would be appealing to Tweens, Y Gens, Baby Boomers, and Active Seniors. Explore more and focus in on sub-audiences. For example, *E Harmony* people interested in safely dating online, *Monster* for job seekers, Ping for all golfers. Go deeper: Lady Fairway shoes for women golfers. What audience do you address? Can you be a leader in a sub category?

V.I.P. Owning a word is not just for big companies. It's even more important for small companies. A great example of the power of owning a word on the neighborhood level: a dry-cleaner came to me wanting help in finding a word that could be the fulcrum of his marketing strategy. The word phrase I arrived at was *Free Home Pick-Up and Delivery*. They planted their stake and claimed they were number one in *Free Home Pick-up and Delivery*. The unique selling proposition was: why waste gas and time to take items to the dry-cleaner and then have to go and pick them up? We do it for you. Just place the soiled clothes in a bag outside your door; we will pick them up and return them within two days and they will arrive cleaned and pressed. Then we drilled deeper in our word search and added the word "environmental" to the word cleaners. Besides professing to be number one in *Free Home Pick-up and Delivery*, the "halo effect" came into play and the marketplace accepted their claim to be the first environmental cleaner.

The results have been amazing! His "word ownership" has resulted in four positive business-changing benefits: First and foremost, a whole new business opportunity unveiled itself. Second, he has set himself apart from all local dry-cleaners. Third, because of the mobility, his market area has increased significantly. Fourth, He can dramatically expand his business without the expense of opening more retail outlets. Remember, none of these benefits would have fallen to the company owner had he not searched for a word-phrase. You must do the same!

If you want to be a leader in a category, you can't own the same or a similar attribute as your competition; you have to be different. Similar won't do it. For example, Gatorade and Red Bull are both refreshing drinks. Gatorade chose the word-phrase *Official Sports Drink*. Red Bull defined itself as the *Number One Energy Drink*. Now there are some taglines that are very clever, but they are not benefit-oriented. Like the Taxidermist who chose the word *Stuff*. Or the Obstetrician whose tagline phrase is *Push, Push, Push*. The owner of the muffler shop who chose *We Hear You Coming*. The word choice *Stuff* doesn't set him apart from other Taxidermists. *Push, Push, Push* doesn't say what the doctor is going to do for you. *We Hear You Coming* identifies a problem, not a solution. Just because you can hear a customer coming doesn't make you a category leader. These are *taglines*, not ownership words.

If you establish yourself as the category leader, when your competitors try to copy you all they will be doing is reinforcing your number-one status. Regardless of reality, people perceive the leader's product in the category to be superior. It doesn't matter if your new product is better; marketing is a battle of perceptions. Differentiate or Die. Customer satisfaction has become a "given," not a differentiator.

If at first you can't seem to think of what you can be number one in, keep thinking because you can always become number one in some category or make up your own. For example, let's say that your product category is razor-blades. The competition is brutal. Gillette is a dominate number one. The challenge is: how do you become number one in that category? The answer is, you can't! So, you must create a category where you can proclaim *your* product as number one. Here is what I would do: I would sit down and make a list of the all the beneficial attributes of my razor blades. Word phrases like "great shave" and "using the technology of the future" mean nothing. Gillette could say the same thing but with more impact. "Safe and Smooth" are already taken. What they don't advertise is the number of shaves per blade. So you become number one in most shaves per blade. In that case, you name the company *Save-a-Blade* and follow it with the tagline *"Up to two-hundred shaves from a single blade."*

I would also strongly suggest that, as an individual, you also own a word. In my case, I chose the words *Master Persuader.* Now don't get me wrong, I don't go around calling myself that, but it's a positive mental image builder for me.

As I go around the world lecturing, I'm always asked: "Isn't what you're saying about owning a word-phrase the same as discovering your Unique Selling Proposition?" No, it's not! The USP is the description of the category you're number one in. To me, the USP is the persuader within the category. First comes "word ownership" and then the blueprint of how to deliver the unique sales message. The USP may change, but the ownership of the word does not.

Once the leadership in a category has been established, there are six secrets for drafting and implementing your unique selling proposition:

1. When you have positioned your company as Number One in the new category, the Unique Selling Proposition should promote the category. In essence, you have no competition. You don't have to establish that your product is better. When you're the leader, you don't have to climb mountains of disparity.

2. When your product is new and new to a category, it's often better to tell the prospect what the product is not, rather than what it is. *Horseless Carriage* is a name that allowed the public to position the concept against the existing mode of transportation. A computer has to accept what you put in it. The mind does not. In fact, it's quite the opposite. It tends to reject new information that doesn't compute; it only accepts new information that matches its current state of mind. It must relate to the old.

3. Once you have settled on the category and the USP, you need to test it. You may think what you came up with is the best thing since sliced bread. You may be right; nevertheless, you must test it. Basically, you want to find out if the *Dogs Like The Dog Food*. Without testing, it's like writing a marketing plan with a broken pencil . . . it's pointless.

4. People think that the more detailed the plan, the safer the new venture or a new product is. The opposite is true. There are only two kinds of businesses: those that prefer planning over testing and those that make money. The longer you plan, the more money you spend. You can sometimes go into a business too quickly, but you can never start testing too soon. First, you must find out if your venture is going to be profitable. Profitability is a guide to what you should be doing. Second, you must avoid ventures where you are not sure if the target market wants and needs your product. The only way to know is to **test . . . test . . . test!** It need not be expensive, but it will be costly if you don't.

5. The USP has to be flexible in that you might have to strategically re-position the way you communicate your sales message. The main reason why is that the Y Generation is big enough to hurt boomer brands. *Nike* sales are tumbling and *Levi Strauss & Company* is no longer the hippest jean-maker on the shelf. These kids are not baby boomers. They have totally different buying patterns. They are not so much brand-oriented as they are into what's hip, trendy and new. Understanding the Y Gen is a marketing snapshot into the future. Your message copy needs to win their hearts and wallets. Your USP has to be internet-friendly and flexible. Your unique selling position should include a social network platform strategy.

6. Put *Wow* in your know-how. Your USP should be benefit-driven. In a new category it's important to plant your flag and say you know more, you can do it better and it's new because the market has changed. *Claim* without shame!

Law of Predictability

Once your "word ownership" is agreed upon, the USP is clearly defined, and initial testing has been completed, then further behavioral research is needed for you to know exactly how your customers are going to act and what questions they will ask. The research will quickly let you find out what the frequently-asked-questions will be. You'll also know what challenges you'll be facing. Once their questions and reactions become predictable, then you script a sales presentation that has ready answers to control the entire selling syllogism. I call that phrase the "Law of Predictability." If you want to be successful in any endeavor, you need to know in advance the best answer to any question that you may be asked or any question you will ask. So that you never violate the Law of Predictability, never, never ask a question you don't already know the answer to. A great example of violating that marketing axiom was when the prosecuting attorney Johnny Cochran asked O.J. to try on the glove without knowing the predictable outcome. That faux pas became Johnny Cochran's mantra: *If it doesn't fit, you must acquit.* Adhering to the Law of Predictability, you will always be in control. It will be your insurance policy to protect yourself from being surprised and compromised.

This Law of Predictability emerged from my MBA Thesis. It's of paramount importance that you make sure you can predict what the prospect's response will be. This is best illustrated in the predictability of telling of a joke. There are four working elements: First, the joke has to be funny (the product has to be good). Second, the joke must be easily told (the message must be easily repeated). When the funny joke is told, what is the predictable outcome? The person to whom the joke is told will laugh. Third, the storyteller is rewarded with the innuendo in his mind that he's perceived to be a funny guy (the company is recognized as being a valued provider). Fourth, the person who just laughed perceives that he, too, can be a funny guy like Steve Martin if he just repeats the joke (word-of-mouth will spur the product on).

It's the octane of praise and acceptability that drives a joke or spurs word-of-mouth. When someone recommends a movie, a product or a service, they are praised for making the recommendation. It's this nuance catalyst that drives PR.

The First Commandment, *Thou Shall Own a Word*, is the most-violated law. The business sinner says things like: "I don't have time to find a word" or "I'd rather write a comprehensive business plan and let my agency pick a word." "How do you test a word or a USP?" "Besides, it costs too much." Over 50 years I have heard all the excuses and have seen them fail. It's of paramount importance that you burn your way into consumers' minds with the word you own. Remember, it's better to be first in the prospect's mind than first in the marketplace. What you choose to do with that insight is up to you. However, I guarantee you this: if you commit to searching until you find a category you can become number one in, you will be hugely successful.

Once you own a word, you now need to own an *"Elevator Pitch,"* a thirty-to-sixty-second sound byte meant to say it all. Sounds easy enough, yes? No, especially when the experts tell you it must be introductory, memorable, benefit-laden, unique, catchy, succinct, meaningful, humorous and professional. Geez, that's a lot to accomplish in a few seconds. On the other hand, who knows more about the business than you? Who has more passion and zeal than you? Who has more knowledge? You guessed it . . . no one.

Some Suggestions:

1. Let your voice show your enthusiasm. If you love it, show it.
2. Focus on them, not you. No one cares how many computers you own. They care about what's in it for them.
3. Begin with a phrase that is humorous, provocative or mysterious. Make the listener ask for more. Here are a few good ones I found:

   *IRS Agent: "I'm a government fund-raiser."
   *Private Pilot: "I shrink the globe."
   *Lawyer: "I empower the powerless."

Do not deliver your elevator speech as if you are reading from a script; it should sound relaxed, conversational and spontaneous, even if you have to practice it for hours! After delivering your speech, it's a great idea to give the listener something that makes you even more memorable and reinforces your message. Now this doesn't have to be something expensive or fancy, just clever. For instance, if you're the private pilot in the example above, you might want to hand people tiny globes complete with your contact information.

4. Try beginning or ending your elevator speech with a question. It sets up a dialogue with the prospect. Here's an example of what not to say (notice the number of times "I" is used): "I help small businesses sell their products. I have the skill set to increase sales. I know it sounds like marketing, but what makes me unique is that first and foremost, I am a storyteller. I also have a technical art, writing and design background, which I combine to tell your story in a special, get-their-attention way."
No one cares about you! They only want to know what you can do for *them*. If you want your elevator pitch to be on the same wave length, be on the same wave length as the potential customer. You must air your elevator pitch on the customer's favorite radio station. That's right! *WII-FM* (What's In It For Me).

Because I offer three different business services, I have three different elevator pitches: one for video-production, another for focus-group research and the third for marketing. Here is an example of my marketing elevator speech. This pitch plays well on *WII-FM*.

Are you aware that most American small business owners are largely unsuccessful because they believe that marketing is just another word for advertising? Would you agree? Whether they say yes or no has little effect on the rest of the pitch. Working with our clients, we create and integrate marketing solutions that go beyond just advertising. We strive to make one media dollar perform like three dollars. Wouldn't you like to have that kind of media performance ratio? (You now have the prospect answering in the affirmative). Now it's your turn to create your own elevator pitch.

Conclusion: **There is always a way for you to be Number One.**
There was a poignant TV commercial that dramatized the fact that if you

can't dribble a football, then change your perception. The commercial opens with a six-year-old who is wearing a baseball cap and a team jersey. With a bat and ball in hand, he declares aloud: "I'm the greatest hitter." He tosses the ball up in the air and with a mighty swing, he swats and misses. Strike One! Again he states: "I'm the greatest hitter." Like Casey at the bat, he takes another mighty swing. The bat and ball don't meet and the ball plops onto the ground. Strike Two! Again he calls out: "I'm the greatest hitter." The boy takes a practice swing, grins and tosses the ball high up in the air. The ball and the bat don't meet. Strike Three! He looks down dejectedly, his shoulders slumping. He pauses for a moment; then he looks up with a grin. He calls out: "I'm the greatest pitcher!" **There is always a way for you to be Number One!**

2nd Commandment:
Thou Shall Bless Google's Triad

Everyone wants to be organically ranked number one by Google. But only a few know the secret of how to get to the top ten in ranking. The secret is found in Google's Triad Ranking Algorithm. I will be unveiling that secret, but first I want you understand how clicks are distributed on any given search engine results page. Research shows that the number one sponsored link at the top of the page generates only 2% to 3% of all the clicks. If you're the number one *paid sponsor* on the right-side bar, your click result will range from 1.5% to 2%. If you achieve the first *organic position*, it's estimated you will receive 41-45% of all the searches. The second *organic position* ranking will generate 11% to18%. Do the math: being first in organic results will be twenty-two times more productive than paying to be number one in the top paid sponsored listings. Even the second organic position will be ten times more productive than a number *paid* listing.

Furthermore, despite what you may have been told, Google Adwords only receive 4% to 5% of the total available clicks. In other words, if one hundred people perform a search on Google only five will click on a paid listing. But don't get me wrong, I still believe that all forms of paid traffic are worthy considerations, especially during the testing and start-up phases of a business. My advice to my clients is to shift the bulk of their focus on SEO(Search Engine Optimization). There are two reasons why:

#1 Reason: Organic Traffic is Growing. Paid is Declining!
#2 Reason: Organic Traffic is FREE! (Enough said).

To substantiate my case, let's take the keyword "dog training" and analyze the distribution of actual clicks in a thirty-day period. To begin, you go to the "Traffic Estimator," a very powerful tool inside of Google Adwords that will give you an estimate of the traffic that will be coming to your site. In this case, I told the "Traffic Estimator" to assume I am in position 1 to 3. The estimation was 1.25.

DOG TRAINING
Local Monthly Searches 1,500,000
Estimated Ad Position 1.25
Estimated Daily Clicks 447
Percentage of all clicks .89%

To calculate the percentage of all clicks:

1. You multiply the number of estimated daily clicks by thirty to get the number of monthly clicks you can expect: 447 x 30 = 13,400 clicks.
2. Then you divide the monthly clicks, 13,400, by the total of local monthly searches for "Dog Training,"1,500,000, and you get 0.89%. There you have it.
3. Google's own "Traffic Estimator" tool is telling you you'll probably get less than 1% of the total available traffic, even if you bid up to one of the top three positions. Not too exciting is it? Plus, it's very expensive.

Where are all the clicks going? Answer: the first Organic position (ie, non-sponsored listing) receives 41% to 45% of the available traffic. The second Organic position will receive 11% to 18%. The second Organic listing will receive ten to twenty times more traffic than the top paid listing. The number three Organic position is getting two to three more click results than the number #1 paid positions. Even at Organic position ranking of number ten, you are generating the same click results as the sponsored listing. But you don't have a cost. Just to put that into perspective . . . if you're getting one-hundred clicks a day from Adwords, my clients' whose ranking reaches number one organically are getting one thousand to two-thousand clicks a day. Most importantly, their traffic is free.

When Google Adwords first came on the scene in 2004, clicks on the sponsored links went through the roof. Paid listing received as much as 30%. The reason for the activity was Google users didn't know there was a difference between the Organic listing on the left and the paid listings on the top and on the left. In 2008 the paid results percentage dropped to 10.5%. In 2009 it lowered again to 7.5%. 2010 paid results were 1-5%. While experts may argue over the exact percentage, none of that really matters. What really matters is that the percentage of clicks to sponsored search listings are on the decline, and few expect it to rebound.

It amazes me when a marketing director of a start-up company tells me he/she wants to launch a banner blitz. In the early days of the internet, banner ads ruled online marketing. But as internet users became more and more familiar with banner ads, click-through rates plummeted and the medium took a massive hit. Today banner ads are not effective, a waste of money. VIP: There are two points I want to make here. First, to be successful in marketing, you must be double current so that you'll not be blindsided by banner blindness or any other change in the market place. Way too many times, I observe executives running banners ads and other paid programs because that's what their competitors are doing. Second, no matter your age, you can't stop learning. I'm in my seventies and still very successful because I stay current. I encourage you to be an active learner.

SEO professionals would have you believe that getting ranked is a painful process that should only be attempted by experienced professionals. Not so! If you're current, you'll know that, with Google's most recent ranking algorithm, it is actually quite easy to slide onto the first page of Google if you follow my instructions. The core of Google's listing algorithm is made-up of three primary variables. They are:

1. Content (keywords, domain name mega tags, etc.)
2. Links (inbound, outbound, authority, affiliates etc.)
3. Activity (traffic, RSS subscriptions, comments updated etc.)

I realize that most SEO purists may shun my Triad concept and called it overly simplistic, but I would challenge them to come up with a new Google algorithm variable that does not fall into one of these three core variables. Getting ranked is really only about doing three things:

1. Getting quality, original content (all you want practically for free)
2. Generating a handful of quality links (costs almost nothing)
3. Generating Traffic (some human activity, no spam)

The key is you must do all three. Leave out even one of the Triad, or get them out of order and you won't achieve your Organic listing goal. To understand the importance of the Ranking Triad, you need to understand where Google has come from and the changes they made to their ranking algorithm over the last ten years: From 1998-2003 *Links* ruled. Essentially, they just counted the number of inbound links coming to the site, applied a quality or a page-ranking score to each link and the sites with the most quality inbound links got rated the highest. Obviously, it's a little more complicated than that, but you get the idea.

In 2003, when Google introduced *Adsense* (*http://google.com/services_tour/index.html*), they switched their ranking algorithm to favor content. For *Adsense* publishers, this was great news because they no longer had to worry about generating all those pesky inbound links. The pendulum swung from *Links* to *Content*. Just create some half-way decent content on a niche topic and Google would reward you with nearly instant ranking. It wasn't long before the spammers realized how easy it was to throw an insane amount of content to advance ranking.

In 2006 to early 2010 *Links* ruled again. A link-centric algorithm was better than its content-centric predecessor at reducing the amount of spam pages in the search results.

It didn't take long before black hat SEO pros realized that they could fake the number of inbound links using totally automated tools. So, once again, Google needed to act and act they did.

In the summer of 2010, Google made what I believe will be its last algorithm shift in a very, very long time. To put it simply, Google is now factoring *Activity* more heavily into their ranking equation. (Remember, the third piece of the ranking triad is Activity). In other words, great content and all the links in the world don't mean squat if your page remains unchanged for days and weeks at a time. *Links* and *Content* may get you temporary rankings, but if you want to stay there, you will need *Activity*.

Content and *Links* are just too easy to game and Google recognized this, which is why they won't bother ranking a new site until it gets some traffic, even if the content is decent and the site is getting a steady flow of inbound links. *Activity* is the octane that will ignite a site's ranking.

Google has learned its ranking lesson and will no longer weigh one of the Triad's categories over the others. Nor should you! The new algorithm will now evaluate all three, but in the sequence I set forth earlier. It's of paramount importance that you meet the requirements for each category, respecting the order below. Do not alter the positioning. When completed, you will be ranked.

1. Content   (keywords, domain name, mega tags, etc.)
2. Links   (inbound, outbound, authority, affiliates etc.)
3. Activity (traffic, RSS subscriptions, comments updated etc.)

In conclusion: Here's a basic overview of the steps:

I encourage you put the following four body-copy tips into practice (they're all pretty easy and straightforward). You'll not only save yourself a great deal of money, but it will also increase your chances of getting highly-qualified traffic and, best of all, the traffic will be free!

Step 1: Write your page copy so it's attractive to the search engines. It's a mistake to think you can get better rankings by using your keywords more. Here are some simple tips for writing search-engine optimized body copy:

- Ensure your search term appears in the first few words of the headline of your page.
- Ensure your search term appears once in every block of one-hundred twenty-five words of body-copy and subheadings. It can appear anywhere in the block, (with the exception of the very first one, where it should be in the first ninety characters).
- Include at least one HTML link which contains your search term in the link copy. The easiest way to do this is to have a link at the bottom of the page linking to the top.

Step 2: Begin by building a Content site. Twelve articles are typically enough. I would recommend you create Activity via paid sources and social media to give your site a "pulse". And a pulse is all it needs. Side note: Don't start driving links until your site is getting some traffic. That's a dead giveaway to Google that there are serious shenanigans going on. After all, it doesn't make sense that a site that receives almost zero activity would have thousands of inbound links. Remember, Google is monitoring human activity through their own proprietary tools (ie: Google Analytics, Chrome, Feed Burner, etc.). Here's a trick you should consider: focus all your human activity through Google's propriety channels, making it appear like your site is receiving more activity than it really is.

Step 3: Next, I recommend that you pepper in a few inbound links. Thanks to the onslaught of link brokers, this is incredibly easy to do. For most markets, fifty to one-hundred links is all you need as long as those links come from quality, authoritative sites.

Step 4: We all know that back links are very powerful when it comes to increasing a site's ranking on Google and other major search engines. But many site owners don't realize just how easy it is to get free back links from classified ad sites. Here, in my opinion, are the top classified ad sites that have proven to bring in long-term, high-quality back links.

1. FastTrafficMachine.com
2. usfreeads.com
3. classiedadz.com
4. craigslist.org
5. kijiiji.com
6. domesticscale.com
7. backpage.com
8. oodle.com

Conclusion: Now you know more than most professors teaching in an MBA program. Again, you saved tuition money. When you follow the three steps of the Triad, Google gets what they want: Content, Inbound Links and Measurable Activity. You get Ranked!

MARKETING RELATIONSHIPS IN TRANSITION

This is a very important page for it gives you a clear, concise picture of what is evolving in marketing. Customer buying decisions are also changing. For example: According to Reuters, only 14% of the people believe what a company says about their product or service, whereas 58% of consumers will trust a stranger's recommendation. Take time to read and evaluate each transition as it's a picture of the future!

Subjects	*Old Marketing*	*New Marketing*
Strategy	Top-down strategy imposed by senior management	Bottom-up strategy builds on winning ideas and customer input
Hierarchy	Information is organized into media channels to suit the advertiser	Information is available on demand by keywords to suit users
Sales Pitch	Monologue	Two-way Conversation
Print	Newspaper	Blogs, Social Media
Information	Yellow Pages	Google
Attitude	I'll tell you	Ask Me
Customers	Serve any customer	Serve profitable customers
Payment	Cost per Thousand(CPM)	Return on Investment (ROI)
Relationships	Get New Customers	Keep Old Customers
Commercials	Television, Radio	YouTube
Prospects	Rolodex	Facebook on Steroids

SOCIAL MEDIA CURRENCY: CONTENT—TRUTH—VALUE!

3rd Commandment:
Thou Shall Know What's Hotter Than Hades

The New York Times states that "*Mobile-Marketing* is the hottest sales lead-generator on the planet." You need to know why they made that claim. To begin, *Mobile-Marketing* is not ads on buses; it's *Biz-Texting*. With three billion cell phones worldwide, business owners can now text special offers, coupons or incentives. It's marketing on steroids because the text message read rate is 94%. Here's how this medium works: Customers can text advertisers for bargains and discounts by texting a *Short Code* (also known as short numbers, special telephone numbers significantly shorter than full telephone numbers) that can be used to address SMS and MMS messages from mobile phones or fixed phones. Texting allows advertisers to instantly reach customers with special offers and incentives which, in turn, creates immediate income for them. *Short Codes* are short cellular phone numbers, often five to six digits, to which you attach a keyword. When a person texts in to take advantage of the offer, the caller's cell phone number is captured and the advertiser smiles, for he now knows not only the cell number but he has been given permission to call the person back.

Immediacy: Text messages are typically read within four minutes of dispatch. Emails and direct mail can't compete in response time.

Advertise your keyword on all printed promotions and simply hand out to your customers!

Customers text your KEYWORD to 41513

They receive a text ad offer or incentive from you.

Customers come back to redeem your special offer.

You probably became aware of mobile-marketing when American Idol said you could vote for your favorite by simply texting the word VOTE, which is the Keyword to the Short Code cellular number. The same is true with voting for your favorite on Dancing With the Stars. You would type the keyword "Star" and text it to the short code cellular number. When mobile-marketing was introduced to American Idol in 2003, it was a relatively new medium. No longer. AT&T announced that, in 2009, seventy-eight million messages had texted in their vote at 99 cents. No wonder Simon Cowell was smiling.

Short-Code Examples:

To drive ticket sales, the Anaheim Ducks' Hockey Team rolled out a mobile-marketing promotion that engaged fans and their cell phones. Guests can send in pictures of themselves and some of them end up on the arena's big screen. There is also a *Guess that Duck* game that fans can play on their cell phones. On non-Ducks' game days, young fans will receive text alerts, text-to-win games and voting by text promotions. The National Hockey League has been pushing mobile-marketing to generate a younger fan base by using text games and cell phone uses and it's working.

KFC cooked up a very aggressive mobile-marketing campaign to promote its Hot Wings. This bucket is full of short-code promotions. They had their short-code number everywhere, and I mean *everywhere*, on table tents, coffee cups, napkins, in print ads, billboards or anything breathing. No one could ever call KFC's marketing director a "chicken."

Nothing is sacred when it comes to mobile-marketing. Proctor & Gamble really pushes the envelope when it comes to *Charmin*. Very few people know or care that *Charmin* is the number-one toilet paper. But P&G does. To that end, they are sponsoring a website and iphone application that helps consumers find the cleanest public restrooms worldwide. When a person texts to find out what sit or squat restroom is best, P&G captures the person's email address and acquires an opt-in.

My reason for telling you about these texting strategies is to encourage you to make sure that there are short-code promotions in your marketing arsenal.

Retail Codes is the oldest of the codes. First surfaced in the 80's to price products in supermarkets. Now that bar code is on all retail products.

Online Coupon Codes allows a company to send a coupon to a person's cell phone. The coupon is redeemable when shown or printed out at the advertiser's retail outlet.

Quick-Response Codes (QR) could be the next advertising wave of the future. QR codes are common in Japan where it was created by Toyota subsidiary, Denso-Wave. The QR code is one of the most popular types of two-dimensional barcodes. Users take a photo of a QR code with their cell camera phone and the photo will redirect them to a web page. You will need to download the applicable app to make it work.

These funky codes can be scanned with your iPhone, a co-worker's Blackberry, or that personality-impaired tech guy's android apparatus. Scanning a QR Code allows you to obtain instant answers and links you directly to whatever you may need.

Imagine pointing your cell phone's camera at the QR bar code on a For Sale sign in front of a house and having immediate access to all the information on that house. Or scanning the QR code on a movie poster and immediately getting a trailer for the movie right on your phone. It's all possible with *Quick-Response Code*.

Top 4 Uses for the Quick-Response Code

Get Informed

Picture this: You're walking along a nature trail and you spot a really cool area with a sign post that has a QR code on it. You whip out your phone, scan it, and instantly you're able to gather information about the trail, the park, the flora and fauna of the location, park and trail history and other interesting spots to visit.

Take that one step further and imagine you've traveled to a new city. Instead of following a crowded tour, you can self-guide yourself with the use of QR codes you find along your journey. By doing this, you make your trip an adventure of your own rather than taking the route and pace that most tourists follow. The availability of acquiring information within seconds is something that QR codes are incredibly efficient at and will be increasingly productive in the future.

Ta Da! Instant Action

QR Codes can direct an otherwise passive viewer to take immediate action, make a purchase, register for an event, or take a survey. Our on-demand society already has a jam-packed schedule that makes even the most emotionally-charged buyer difficult to reach unless you can give them a way to take swift action now. Here's another QR call-to-action powerful use. For example: You're deciding what movie to go so you to take a picture of the QR bar-code that appears on a movie poster or in an advertisement and a movie trailer comes up on your cell phone.

A Traffic Highway to Websites

Instead of posting a long website address that your audience is likely to forget by the time they get to their computer, place a QR Code on your printed piece. Whether it's an advertisement, direct mail, business card, flyer, or exterior street signage, your potential consumer can immediately gain access to what your company is about, what you're promoting, and you can nudge them to act now instead of the dreaded "maybe later." And to top it off, you can track and analyze the results of your printed pieces. After all, if you can't measure it, you can't improve it or repeat it. Marketing shouldn't be guesswork.

Turn a Printed Catalog into a Storefront

What if your customers could check inventory and purchase 24 hours a day right from your printed catalog? QR Code your catalog and they can! Coding your catalog doesn't limit a customer depending on their time zone, company business hours, or their busy schedule. Not only does this help increase usability, but it also expands the productivity of your potential sales. So whether your shopper is an early bird or a night owl, the opportunity is there! In the United States, Ralph Lauren's Polo is pioneering the use of this technology in the fashion world. They are turning advertisements into storefronts.

Microsoft "Tag" Bar Codes

Tags connect real life and the digital world. By just scanning the "tag" with their smart phone, it gives customers instant access to your website, YouTube videos and virtual tours.

There are more cell phones in the US than TVs and computers combined, and more text messages were sent yesterday than there are people on the planet. More ad dollars will be shifting away from traditional marketing methods and on to mobile advertising ($500 billion worldwide). *Mobile-Marketing* is the hottest advertising trend in history, with over two billion potential customers.

According to the Mobile-Marketing Association in 2010, 57% of the large companies will use text and multi-media messaging to reach into their consumers' pocket books via their mobile phones. On the other hand, less than **6%** of small and medium-size businesses have a *Common Short Code* texting component. Recent studies show that 66% of consumers search goods online.

The revenue opportunities for *Common Short Code* can be separated into four different categories: marketing, advertising, entertainment, and commerce. Each has separate objectives, but all depend on instituting a complete solution that incorporates domestic acceptance of CSC, a premium billing capability and valuable content offerings.

The number one question I'm asked is: "Won't text messaging become cluttered with spam texts and turn the new marketing wave into a ripple?" No, because the customer is texting you and you are automatically prepared to answer. To prevent the deadly effects of spam texting, I recommend the double *"opt-in"* method. Here's how it works: An advertiser inserts his short code (cellular number with the keyword) into all of his/her collateral, advertisements, and broadcast commercials. A potential customer hears or reads of the special offer, discount or information the advertiser is offering and if the person wants to avail themselves of the offer, then they text in. At this time the caller's cell phone number is captured. Once the advertiser receives the first opt-in text, there is an immediate response sent to the caller, asking the person if he wants to receive information about the offer. If so, please click "Yes." They always click "Yes," because they wanted the information in the first place. Once the person answers "Yes," the advertiser now has two permission opt-ins, allowing the seller to contact the potential customer, plus he has captured the caller's cell phone number.

Be very careful. Many would argue that it could be the beginning of a steep decline in human relations and face-to-face communication. Others see it as another step forward in the ever increasing wave of technology and as a tool to make our lives more productive. Whichever camp you might fall into, there is no denying that it is more than just a simple fad that will go away anytime soon. It's here to stay, like it or not. That being said, many savvy business people have found ways to profit from this latest trend by using mobile phone advertising.

In the world of marketing and advertising, mobile phone advertising in the United States is still in its infancy. So new, as a matter of fact, that it was really unknown until recently whether it could be a profitable venture or not. Well, the results are in and not only has it proved to be a wildly profitable form of marketing, it has exceeded all manners of expectations. Many marketers are beginning to focus more time and money on this explosive form of advertising and changing their entire focus and direction to capitalize on this while it is still so young. Just look at happenings on the internet by some of the largest businesses in the world and the focus on mobile websites geared directly at the smart phone technology market. This new focus is opening up a whole new world to be accessed with ease never before imagined. It only makes sense that these same businesses would also direct so much energy into advertising to these people they are so drastically trying to reach.

It is safe to say that mobile phone advertising will only continue to grow for a long time as well as change course with new data made available. It begs the question, just as every new big marketing idea does, what's next? I personally can't wait to find out!

The Common Short Code market in the United States represents an exciting opportunity for anyone, including media, entertainment, consumer packaged goods, advertising, or technology companies to connect nearly two-hundred million wireless subscribers to their goods and services using interactive applications never before available in the wireless industry.

Social Media Marketing is "Hot"

Don't wait until it clears up in your mind. For the majority of small & medim size buizreses owenrs Social Medea is unchragadted waetr. If u can raed this it's a graet anology for makpng the poient that Social Medea will become claer to yu, in a very shrot time. So strat to learn today! Facebook and YouTube have 500 mililon custemrs of yoers . . . Procrastination is juet keeiping up wtih yestehdy.

According to rsceearch at Cmabridge Uinervitisy, it deosn't mttaer in what orderb the ltters in a word r the only the imprrmoetnt thing is that the first and lsat lttee be ni the righit pclae. The rset can be a total mses and you can still raed it wouthit b problem. This is bcuseae the humnn mnid deos not read erey lteter by istlef, but the word as a wlohe.

Moral: Don't wait until it clears up in your mind. Jump in right now. Once you understand how social media can build your business, you'll wonder why you hadn't acquired that knowledge sooner. The good news is you're not alone. Small businesses are still behind the online curve, but you won't be!

Unfortunately, I hear way too often, "Don't bother me with that Social Media Marketing stuff. It's for kids." Not so. Why would this 74-year-old kid like myself say that's not so? It's because, in this tech-driven age, you're not going to heat-up your business unless you integrate social media into your marketing mix. Social media is not a fad; it's growing at warp speed. It took radio thirty-eight years to reach fifty-million listeners. It took Television thirteen years, the Internet four years and the iPod just three years to reach fifty-million people.

According to the Nielson Co., social networking takes up 22.7% of a user's computer time.

There are over five-hundred-million users on Facebook.
There are ninety-three-million users on Twitter.
There are eighty-five-million users on Linkedin.

How many hours a week are spent on social sites?

A. 4:4 hours
B. 2:1 hours
C. 4:6 hours

The answer is 4.6 hours; that's 18.4 hours a month; that's the equivalent of 2.3 days a month. How many hours do people spend on Facebook in a month?

A. 6:48
B. 8:45
C. 7:01

The answer is 7:01 hours. Facebook has 25% of all web pages in the United States. What many business executives don't know is that Facebook has a Business Page. At first it was called a Fan Page. Now it is identified as *I Like*. The reason for the new name is because it defines what people do. You post relevant business information and if a reader likes what you wrote, he/she will click the *I Like* button. The page is for business information about you and your company. It's a business resume; not a social site You only invite people who are relevant business friends.

According to the Mobile-Marketing Association (MMA), 59 % of mobile users surveyed said they used their mobile phone to shop for Christmas discounts and sales.

Let's begin with Social Media Marketing 101

Social networking is a contagious, unavoidable phenomenon that doesn't stop at socialization. More and more organizations are leveraging these sites to effectively market themselves. This isn't news to you because, clearly, you don't operate your business from a cave. Whether or not you find social networking to be daunting, you must consider it to be a key component in your marketing plan.

Utilizing social networking sites is more than just creating a profile for your business and hoping someone sees it. It's about giving consumers and potential clients the chance to see the human side of your organization. You're no longer a big corporation being led by a team of robots; you're a friend on their friend's list. Like most things in life, you will get out what you put in.

The flexibility that comes with social media is invaluable. Website changes can be costly, depending on what's necessary, but a social networking profile can be altered in seconds. You can feature links to your website, videos and pictures. The age group that needs to become knowledgeable with this new media is the *older* executive who is fifty and older. It's of paramount importance that he/she understands the dynamics of social platform marketing. There's a very important corollary that is applicable to the X and Y generations. Heed this advice well: Social Marketing is not a marketing fulcrum. It's nothing more than an important tool to be integrated into your total marketing mix.

Twitter De, Twitter Dumb

Don't become dumb when it comes to *"Tweets."* They are small messages, but they can bring big results. One-hundred-forty characters may not seem like enough space to get your message across but you can use these "mini-blogs" to drive traffic elsewhere via a link.

You don't have a *Twitter* account yet? Are you venturing into the online of social networking? No worries. It's all so new that you can't be that far behind the early adopters. Way too many business people wrongfully think that twittering is a teens' media. It may have been, but now it's a powerful marketing media. "Jane just kissed Jack" tweets have evolved into more meaningful content: Sale at Nordstrom's tomorrow—The Fed has raised its rate—Outback has a 2 for 1 dinner!

Twitter is far better than e-mail for reaching the masses. E-mail has become a highly-abused communication and marketing tool. Today, many executives don't even read their emails or the spam filter sends them into the wastebasket in the sky never to seen by a human again. Another problem is: e-mail lists are expensive and most are shopworn. In 2009, Boston College and Harvard stopped distributing e-mail addresses to incoming freshmen. Facebook has made e-mail passé.

Twitter is all about people joining with others. It began as a simple way for one person to immediately, in real time, let others know what they are doing. Today, it's used to notify customers about sales, discounts and promotions.

It soon became clear that just letting your extended family know that you were, at this moment, having corn flakes for breakfast was not where the great value was to be had from *Twitter*. The light bulb went on and it was quickly deducted that if people were to tell their associates and customers what their business was doing in short, interesting messages and the text could be received on the follower's cell phone, it could revolutionize sales lead-generation. And it has!

Celebrity twitter endorsements are already big business in the US, where artists such as Snoop Dogg can earn a reported $3,500 per tweet. Reality TV star Kim Kardashian, who has more than 5.6 million followers, can collect up to $10,000 for tweeting. Celebrities can be great influencers, when they are tweeting. Stars like Jennifer Lopez can get six figures a year, and in some cases six figures a quarter for tweeting about a product they like or they have bought. In the beginning, celebrities were wary about their reputation, about selling out, but when they saw how easy it was to earn up to $5,000 a tweet, they flocked on board.

For example, let's say you have a golf product and a major PGA golfer has signed to endorse your product. That news makes for a great tweet. It's really simple: you go to your twitter account, post this good news and within seconds thousands of your followers will know of the endorsement. The first tweet should be followed by short-burst announcements to provide more insights.

The more twitters you can get to follow you will result in more business opportunities. Many times I hear, "Why would someone follow me?" Easy answer. Because they have come to know that you have great sales and unique products. Say you sell shoes and you want your response to reach anyone within a twenty-mile radius of your business. When someone seven miles away tweets about shoes, your response will automatically send that person information about your big shoe sale. Or maybe you have a sushi bar in Chicago? A potential customer tweets: I want a great sushi dinner. Do you have a special?" You tweet back, "Yes, we do. A two-for-one special." You then explain the special promotion. It's that simple. When someone tweets, they want buying information instantly! When you automatically respond instantaneously you generate a hot prospect who is interested in what you have to sell.

The number one question I'm always asked is, "How do I get people to follow me?" There are companies like Sprout Social, Twitterific and Twitter Hawk that have advance search technology that can help you connect with twitters related to the keywords you choose and the location.

Followers are your customers. Remember, every follower also has followers. It will amaze you how fast your follower base will grow.

Caution:

What happens in Las Vegas stays on Twitter, so be cautious what you tell on-line to your friends. Think Anthony Weider!

YouTube YouTube is the 2nd largest search engine in the world. It contains one-hundred million videos and receives two-billion viewers each day. That's two billion viewers! It's mandatory that you must have your videos and commercials on YouTube, along with traditional broadcast airings. Perhaps the star of the social media is Facebook which added one-hundred million users in just nine months and now has five-hundred million users. Notwithstanding, I'll caution again: don't spend all your direct-marketing dollars on social networking. Do not make it the fulcrum of advertising until the sales results are in!

According to Ad-ology Research, small businesses have to get ready to embrace online video. In the near future, video will over take print. There is no wiser investment of your time than you finding out everything you can about YouTube, for it will level the playing field for your business. It will amaze you how easy it is to register your YouTube account and upload your first video. Begin by going to YouTube. Fill out the simple registration form. Make sure a user name is available. Then click on the sign-up button. YouTube will tell you to go and check your email and find the email from YouTube confirming your email address. It will open a new window on the right side. There is an upload link. Click it to start uploading your first video. Enter a title for the video, a description and mega tags. The mega tags are going to be very important in your Search Engine Optimization Strategy (SEO). Presto! You're a TV producer with your own channel.

LinkedIn

Linkedin reaches over eighty-five million business professionals with an average income of $109,000. LinkedIn is an excellent place to start if you're just starting out using social media for your business. These are business professionals who are expecting to make professional connections, so you need not feel like a fish out of water. Asking for and receiving recommendations from clients and colleagues can up your credibility and open doors.

MySpace

MySpace is an excellent place to advertise as it offers precise targeting of prospects by a number of criteria. You can drill down to find the right prospect demographics. Let's say that you have an offer for a weight-loss product and you decide to target females of any age who just gave birth. Two clicks and you have identified your target audience. Your offer will be exposed to 180,000 prospects for as little as $.02 per click.

Facebook

Facebook has become the new MySpace. When Mark Zuckerberg created Facebook, he never imagined having 500-million users. As discussed, Facebook business page (*I Like It*) offers a great opportunity for millions of eyeballs to look at your company and evaluate how your product or service will benefit them. Currently, you aren't able to recruit fans from your business page, but if you already have a substantial network, and are friends with others who do as well, you'll be able to gather an immediate following. Facebook also allows your business to create ads to drive your business.

Many people miss the marketing magic of Social Media, because it's dressed in overalls and looks like too much work.

What You Need To Be Doing

Your profile on any social networking forum should be engaging, current and personal. Not only will the constant updating of your profile keep people interested, but on sites like Facebook it will keep you on the top of other people's minds. Making your profile personal and engaging will put a human face to your organization and others will feel more comfortable doing business with you.

Build Your Data-Based Network

On most social media sites, you can add others to your network and, in turn, you're added to theirs. On Twitter it isn't automatic that they're following you just because you're following them. However, they will usually return the favor. When looking to add new contacts, search for other people and businesses that have something to offer you and your organization.

Be Topical & Relevant

You can't engage potential customers and clients if you don't create content relevant to them. Post content that pertains to your market and use language they can relate to. Answer questions, post helpful articles and tips, and keep your network informed on upcoming events.

Join Interest Groups

Groups are an excellent way to build your network because you can find people who are interested in the same topical content you are. They also are helpful in gathering information and staying up to date in your industry. Join a group relevant to your organization or, better yet, start your own.

Too Much is Too Much

Consumers will do everything possible to avoid feeling like they're being advertised to. That's why it's crucial when utilizing social media to keep this in mind and respect the consumer. Sending out mass messages is a major "no-no". Not only is it impersonal, but it can be rather annoying to receive what feels like spam on a regular basis. Instead, updating your status or profile will do the trick, especially on Facebook where your friends will actively see these changes or on Twitter where you're being followed.

I regularly check up on other sources of information, and suggest you do the same. There are some really great resources out there and plenty of writers, bloggers and experts willing to share their knowledge. After a while, using social media will become second nature in running your business, but it's important never to forget the personalization that creates lasting partnerships. VIP: If you're successful in making contacts online, it's vital to follow up on a more personal level such as over the phone, a handwritten note or face-to-face meetings whenever possible.

If You Don't Link You'll Sink

The secret to internet success can be summed up in three little words: Link, Link and Link! Consider your social media profiles as traffic conductors to your company website. Posting links to interesting content, landing pages, samples of your work, videos, photos, and surveys will keep your network engaged and will encourage them to become more familiar with your organization or brand. Affiliate Partner's linkage comes in two forms. Referral partners are great at driving traffic to your website. *Value-Added Re*-sellers (VARs) are great at selling on your behalf. Since you pay on performance, referral and VAR programs have a high return. In the end it all comes down to understanding what motivates your affiliate partners and developing incentives that best fit their needs. Link or you will sink!

Conclusion: IT'S BEGINNING TO LOOK A LOT LIKE MOBILE

Embarce the technoalogpy noow, it will clear up . . . It's beter to laen, now thean be behind the onlnie cuvre and fial in the future! If you're not already, you need to become not only a user, but a student of Mobile-Marketing and Social Media. It's an exciting time everyday something is evolving.

If Fred Flintstone returned from Bedrock, you could hear him saying with jubilation: "Apps Dabba Dooo! App is not just the acronym for mobile phone applications, it's a passport for you to build client relationships. It's a powerful communication tool for businesses because it defines a person's search for information. It's all right there and said by the company in the right way.

Talking about Apps. Lady Gaga goes to Farmsville, Who's Lady Gaga? Why would she go to Farmsville? What's Farmsville? Farmsville is a farming social network game that millions and millions play everyday. The game allows members of Facebook to manage a virtual farm by plowing land, planting and harvesting virtual crops. The Farmsville game is also available on the Apple iPhone. The pop icon recognized the power of social communications and Apps to sell her songs. A brilliant "*Blue Ocean*" marketing concept. 62 million active players have to complete tasks to hear one exclusive new track per day.

If your company wants to stay on top, you must stay current with the latest mobile-marketing technologies and not leave it all to your agency or marketing director. You need to understand what the agency is submitting for your approval. It's changing so fast the concepts and strategies are written on chalk boards that can be easily erased so new ones can be added. Advice: To stay abreast of the newest online marketing concepts you must read, search the internet and ask young nerds what's new.

The way you spell Twitter is I.n.s.t.a.n.t. Twitters want their buying information instantly. They are hot to buy. I can hear Jed Clampett saying, "There is money in them there tweets."

If you're the company's Marketing Director, make sure you're both *Old School* and *New School* in your thinking. It's of paramount importance that you study the buying behaviors of the Y generation because they are a snapshot of the future. Most importantly, you must link so you won't sink!

I'll caution you again, don't spend all your direct-marketing dollars on social networking.

"I have it on my iPod"

4th Commandment:
Thou Shall Not Fish for Tunas in a Lake

Effort without direction equals frustration. You can run toward the east as fast and hard as you are capable of and you'll never see a sunset. No matter how hard you try, *you'll never catch a tuna in a lake.* It's amazing how many executives have said to me, "Bill, I don't think you understand. I've purchased the best bait and tackle money can buy." It doesn't matter. *There are no tunas in a lake.* "You have to see my new fishing pole. It's guaranteed to catch a tuna." That may be so, but not in a lake. "Look Would it be less expensive?" Why waste any time discussing the matter. *There are no tunas in a lake.* If you're an executive of a start-up or a small company, you can't afford to waste time because you'll run out of money. It's as if some executives have sound-proof heads.

"I'm not giving up. I'm going to keep fishing here in this lake until a customer shows up." Your persistence is admirable, but futile. Your friends or spouse may think you're very stubborn for not going to the sea to fish, where you'll catch a tuna, but we both know you're not stubborn. You're just not sure where to fish. You're not positive what media bait you should be using. Don't feel bad. You're not alone. Everyone has a fear of the unknown. The tell-tale sign of how fearful you are is measured by the number of excuses you have for not making a change. The fisherman who rejects changing is the architect of decay. I smile when the fisherman says, "I can change. I'll move to another lake." The reasons why people keep fishing for tunas in lakes is two-fold: First, they place probability before profitability. Second, they fail to plan and, if they did plan and the plan failed, they'd fail to plan again. Here is the square-circle. Persistence is the most important element in a plan. You never fail until you give up. On the other hand, closed-ear persistency, when you don't listen to what others are advising, is a company death knell.

Although it may be your nature to passionately test the waters where no one else has gone, it needs to be reeled in when my rule of three is violated.

1. If two or more people tell you that there are no customers in your lake, Listen!
2. If no one else is fishing in the lake, you shouldn't be there either.
3. Let someone else pioneer new fishing holes. Remember, in exploration the second mouse gets the cheese.

This fish story analogy highlights that way too many executives fish for customers in the wrong marketplaces and continue to do so. Even major, well-established companies have, on occasion, fished in the wrong lake, evidenced by what happened to *Coca-Cola Clothing*. Where oh where is *Adidas* cologne? A by-product of *Adidas* running shoes is sweat, not a sweet fragrance.

You don't run newspaper ads to win the hearts and wallets of the Y generation. They don't read. Don't think you're going to reel in Seniors by using PCP marketing. You won't find Seniors swimming in the YouTube ocean, nor are they found tweeting. The majority of today's marketing books and blogs focus in on the Y generation, saying it's where the action is. That's *not* where the money is. Seniors represent the fastest-growing consumer group in America and around the world. You must be aware of their psychographics, for they have evolved to where the only thing that matters to the senior market is if the product or service works. If the product keeps its sales promise, the news will spread fast and you'll have a winner. No wonder Viagra was such smash hit. One senior told another and another. Because seniors are adept in making buying decisions, they like the facts. Symbolism and trendy creative executions leave them cold. (I'm the exception to the rule).

If you're fishing to catch the "Y" generations' business, you must stay current. It's a market unlike any other; it is constantly in a swim mode going from one fad fish hole to another very quickly. There's a line from the movie *The King and I* that says "*By the pupils you shall be taught.*" That is the reason why I teach now and then as an ad hoc professor in the MBA programs at Vanguard and Concordia Universities here in Orange Country, California. I wanted to stay in touch with the thinking of the Y generation. Born after 1980, they comprise one-third of all America. They are starting to pour into the work world with values, aspirations and approaches that differ significantly from their parents and co-workers. The Y generation is big enough to hurt boomer brands by giving them the cold shoulder and big enough to launch rival brands. I cannot stress enough that you must become pro-active in learning about this new wave of customers. Besides you becoming familiar with their buying attitudes, it will be important to have your boomers or yourself mentor the Y gens. It will be amazing what you will learn. Understanding the Y generation is a marketing snapshot into the future.

In the future, "Branding" products in the minds of the Y generation is going to be very difficult, very challenging. Many advertising gurus are saying: "We will make them change." That is so myopic. The ad agency boomers are the ones who are going to have to change. It's important to understand that "buyer behavior' can be transmitted from one Y Gen to another just like a virus. A small number of youthful consumers can ignite a trend and literally kill a brand that has cost millions to be top of the mind.

Recently, I spoke at the Harvard Business Schools Entrepreneurial Conference in Southern California. My subject was the impact that the Y generation is going to have on marketing. One of my fellow panelists who was a 28 year-old, extremely-successful entrepreneur blew my mind when he said he didn't have working hours for his employees. They could come and go as they wished as long as they got their work done. It was his premise that future managers will manage the process not the personnel. I'm too old-school to think that would work in the long run. But it's a provocative insight into the mind-set of the Y Generation. Those Y Gens who get too big for their britches will be exposed in the end.

Conclusion: Don't fish for Tunas in a lake. Never let your persistency turn into stubbornness. Always be willing to listen to other people's evaluations. You don't have to accept their evaluations, but if you dismiss my Rule of Three, it's at your peril.

#1. If two people tell you that there are no customers in your lake, Listen!

#2. Add to it, if no one else is fishing in the lake, you shouldn't be there either.

#3. Let someone else pioneer new fishing holes. Remember, in exploration the second mouse gets the cheese.

The Lake also symbolizes traditional marketing where, in most cases the senior fishes swim. The Ocean represents new-school marketing. It's where the Y Gen Tunas are. If you really want to grow your business, fish both the lake *and* the ocean, but with different customer bait.

Caution: Because MBA curricula focuses on the entrepreneurial sprit, the exploratory and the innovative, it seems to be at odds with old-fashioned common-sense. *Street-smarts* as an answer seems too mundane, too simple. If the entrepreneurial mindset isn't kept in check, it can be very pricey. It becomes insidious without you knowing it. It doesn't matter if you have great *horse sense* you must continually self-evaluate, to make sure none of your marketing strategies are placing *Probability Before Profitability.*

Games With Day Jobs

OnLine games are now being used to market products. A good example is a company called *Steel Hawk*, a manufacturer of electrified latches that had an innovative product but no name recognition. My client's webmaster created a game for customers to play on their website called *Stalk the Steel Hawk*. He took a page out of the *Angry Birds* playbook. Oh, you don't know about *Angry Birds*? Well, it's an online game played by forty-million active users monthly. Players use a slingshot to launch birds at pigs stationed on or within various structures, with the intent of destroying all the pigs on the playfield. In *Stalk the Steel Hawk* the user goes on a photo safari to Shoot the Hawk. Interwoven into the game are marketing points: for example customer service was identified as "*Talk to The Hawk*". Distribution copy: "The Steel Hawk will be *spotted* everywhere." It's a brilliant marketing concept because all the time the gamer is playing, the name Steel Hawk is being burned into top of the mind status.

Another Game Day Job is Game-Based-Learning for business applications. It's about fun, engagement and serious training. Simulations and role-playing are the two key training tools. The game is played in a simulated business environment (e.g. A CRM user support desk, a production line or a realistic sales meeting). If the learner fails or does not quite deliver the desired outcome, then they can try again with a modified approach such as "learning by doing" or "experiential learning." From a training standpoint, the role-playing develops memory hooks: learners not only remember what happened, but also *why* it happened.

Talking about game-training, many years ago (pre-digital) I was one of the first to use a game format to train sales people. It all happened, because of a strange set of events. At the time, Roone Arledge was president of ABC Wide World of Sports. He asked me to produce a pilot for what was supposed to be a humorous sports game. Unfortunately, it turned out not to be a funny show. As a matter of fact, it was terrible. Because he liked me, or he just wanted to get rid of the set, he magnanimously said, "The set is yours. Do whatever you want with it." Picture this, I drive home, my wife Carol greets me with "how did it go, did Roone like the show?" "Not really." She then looked outside and said "What's that big truck doing in our driveway?"

I answered with an embarrassed stutter, "It's the game-show set." You already know what she said and how joyous she was.

Oddly enough, it worked out to be very profitable. I converted the albatross into a Fortune 1000 traveling game show. The format was like the *Family Feud* but instead of families feuding, I would have the company's salesmen competing. The show would play the last day of the convention, because we would ask them questions about what they should have learned at the various sessions. American Express hired us to put the show on at the Manu Kea in Hawaii. The show began with a Hawaiian-shirted audience whooping it up for the Hula Dancers. Then the game was on! When the salesperson gave the right answer, the audience roared with approval. From a training standpoint, this further confirmed in everyone's mind that was the right answer! When a person gave the wrong answer, a big fun buzzer would blare. At that moment everyone in the audience was alerted to what the right answer should have been. It was powerful training tool. You don't need a big set or a big budget; you can do it in-house.

5th Commandment:
Thou Shall Become a Story Teller

Basically, you can engage and persuade people either by: appealing to them with a compelling factual argument or appealing to them with an engaging story. Or, you may use a combination of both. Which way is best? Your customers will tell you by their responses which is best. All else being equal, I favor the combination of facts and storytelling. Hybrids' ads (facts plus stories) take advantage of the fact that we humans have both a rational and an emotional side.

Sales Presentations, like everything else, have evolved through the years. In the era of Willie Loman, the ice-breaker was a joke the salesman told the buyer. With the *Death of the Salesman*, joke-telling died. It was replaced with the *"Benefits-Features Era,"* led by IBM. Salesmen were taught to recite a laundry list of factual features and benefits. IBM thought that their product was so great that the buyer would be overwhelmed and buy immediately, no need for that relationship-building stuff. Many other companies followed suit. What happened? The Buyers got bored! The power shifted to the buyer and he replaced the benefit pitch with "Give me the bottom line and be on your way."

To counter that, it's now the *Hybrid Era* of facts and storytelling. Buyers will listen to a story. Studies show that the most successful salesmen are storytellers who punctuate their stories with compelling facts.

Creating a hybrid argument should be the third step in the creative process. First, the rational argument based on Facts, Second, the Storytelling and Third, the Combination of Both. The reason for the hybrid being in the third position is that you have invested the time to distill the facts and create your stories, so it stands to reason that the hybrid story will be the most convincing.

Storytelling is An Art

It's a skill-set that salespeople need to learn and have in their sales arsenal. Customers are less critical when listening to a story than when listening to a formal sales presentation. The human mood alters when hearing a story. It's like going to the movies; you become engrossed in the story. It's human nature to give a person the benefit of the doubt if you like what they are saying. The customer has the tendency to say in his/her mind: "Hey, this rep isn't trying to high-pressure me to buy his product."

Storytelling differs from sales-closing techniques in that storytelling is a relationship builder. A story is your most powerful tool when your goal is to influence others. Presenting facts alone, without a story, loses the emotional link required for someone to consider what is being said. Great sales people are excellent storytellers. When you tell a story, the customer listens to what you have to say without a defensive mind-set.

It's very important to make it clear when I'm talking about telling a story, I'm not talking about joke-telling. Successful entrepreneurs and professional sales executives can turn an average testimonial into an unforgettable story that has megawatts more electricity than just a factual pitch. Buyers easily become jaded. They have heard it all. Sales champions intuitively sense this, so they use stories, metaphors, anecdotes and parables. Surprisingly, storytelling works really well with the "*just tell me the price*" buyer.

Storytelling is an excellent way to train the less-productive salespeople. Acrostic one-liners don't work. On the other-hand, stories can change a person's behavior. That's the reason Aesop's Fables were told as stories instead of one line admonishments. It's also a great training tool. In Japan, it is customary for a senior worker (called a Sempai) to mentor a younger worker (called a Kohai) on various issues concerning the company's history and culture and how to do the job. The Sempai does much of his informal teaching through storytelling, although nobody calls it that. But that's what it is. Once a younger worker hears the story of what happened to the poor guy who didn't wear his hardhat on the factory floor, he will never forget to wear his hardhat and remember the company's lists of rules.

Here's The How-To for Storytelling

Clients and customers listen to stories with no guards up. It is easier than you think. Everyone has a few stories to tell. For example, you could create a story about a "tragic hero" (an anonymous customer) who overcomes adversity (the current situation) to attain ultimate glory (the desired state, achieved uniquely by your solution/service). The story also needs to be visually intriguing, with humorous iconography. To be effective, you need to write a script and practice it until it becomes second nature. Be excited telling the story. Don't forget to include planned interaction points where you'll engage with the customer to ensure a two-way dialogue.

Another storytelling tack is asking for permission. "May I tell you how I prepared for this meeting?" (you don't have to wait for his reply). I conducted a consumer focus group and here's what it told me" (tell him your findings). Couch the findings in a way that supports your presentations. "One of your competitors (anonymous) failed to heed this advice and here's what happened." If done well, it will tee up a better selling environment.

I strongly recommend you go online and let the mouse do the walking and find out every thing you can about how storytelling can boost sales and make your leadership acumen more productive. Stories have a beginning, a middle, and an end. Just remember this: it's hard to have a moral to the story when there is no story.

I have an array of stories I am prepared to tell, depending on the occasion. The key word is prepared. These are longer stories and told when there is more time, the environment is friendly and you have a captive audience. You must be well-rehearsed, with purpose in mind when you tell a story. I love to tell personal stories that are self-deprecating.

When I enter an executive's office, I immediately scan the pictures that are displayed. It's quick and easy to determine what that person is interested in. Just look around, sailing artifacts, equestrian trophies, golf pictures, these are all tell-tale signs of where his interests lie. (Caution, women rarely like you talking about their personal interests). During the getting-to-know-you opening phase, it's common to ask a few questions about the person's interests. But that's not storytelling!

For example, if the customer is a golf buff, I tell this (well-rehearsed) true story. I begin by saying I'm a terrible golfer. I have found that if it's a story about you, the story is most appealing if it's self-deprecating. It warms the person up to you.

"I'm a terrible golfer. I believe the only win I ever had was against Stevie Wonder. It was close." In 1987 and 1988 I filmed the Dinah Shore Golf Classic for Colgate. Today it's called the Nabisco Open Championship. That experience gave me the opportunity in 1990 to film the U.S. Senior Open at Ridgewood Country Club. It was the year that Lee Trevino beat Jack Nicklaus. The day after the tournament the sponsor invited their customers and me to play the championship course . . . ."

I'm going stop for a moment to explain that the purpose of giving the dates and the facts is to establish the credibility. If that is too detailed for the customer, I go directly into the story. It's very important for you to estimate in your mind how much time you have to tell the short or long versions.

"I'm a terrible golfer. Let me tell you *how* terrible. Many years ago I was filming the U.S. OPEN Senior Championship. It was the year that Lee Trevino beat Jack Nicklaus. The day after the tournament, the sponsor invited their customers and me to play the Championship Course and have one of the professional caddies be our caddie. Well, I'm out there having a great time. My caddie didn't seem to be enjoying it as much as I was.

For some reason he was getting tired walking into the woods to get my balls. We come to the 8th hole and I see a telephone on a tree. I asked him "What's that for?" He said, "You call ahead to order food." I said, "What a great idea! Should I do that?' He said, "The way you play it will be cold!"

That Story always results in a laugh and starts the meeting on a positive up-beat note. It allows me to be in social control. My advice is for you is to draft and rehearse a variety of applicable, true stories. Stories, when told, will result in teeing up what you hope to accomplish.

Also, the occasion and the audience dictate the story to be told. For example: I tell women's groups the *Cracked Pots* story to look beyond their flaws and realize how important they are.

An elderly woman had two large pots. Each hung on the ends of a pole which she carried across her neck. One of the pots had a crack in it, while the other pot was perfect and always delivered a full portion of water. At the end of the long walk from the stream to the house, the cracked pot arrived only half full. For a full two years this went on daily, with the woman bringing home only one and a half pots of water.

Of course, the perfect pot was proud of its accomplishments. But the poor cracked pot was ashamed of its own imperfection and miserable that it could only do half of what it had been made to do. After two years of what it perceived to be bitter failure, it spoke to the woman one day by the stream. "I am ashamed of myself because this crack in my side causes water to leak out all the way back to your house." The old woman smiled, "Did you notice that there are flowers on your side of the path but not on the other pot's side? That's because I have always known about your flaw so I planted flower seeds on your side of the path and, every day while we walk back, you water them. For two years I have been able to pick these beautiful flowers to decorate the table. Without you being just the way you are, there would not be this beauty to grace the house." Each of us has our own unique flaw, but it's the cracks and flaws we each have that make our lives together so very interesting and rewarding. You've just got to take each person for what they are and look for the good in them. Remember to smell the flowers on your side of the path".

When you tell a story, always describe the place and the circumstances in such a way that the audience can feel like they have been there. They can visualize walking with the elderly woman who was carrying the two pots. Read the paragraph below and you'll see just what I mean by vivid descriptions:

For example: I am in the Kuala Lumpur International Airport waiting for someone to arrive. There's a mid-east smell that permeates the airport. It's hot, the air seems to be standing still. There are two women seated across from me. Their faces were shielded by their black Burkas. How hot, I thought, they must be. In contrast, the men were wearing western GQ suits. There are many cultures speaking, but I only heard people speaking English with a huge American accent. I also noticed the predominance of just two colours, silver and blue, matching the steel frames and the painted walls. As I looked out the floor to-ceiling window, I saw a jasmine tree but I couldn't smell the sweet aroma. Mental Imagery makes storytelling interesting and involving.

In my storytelling search, I came across the Sun and the Wind Aesop Fable. To me it had a meaningful moral: that it's better to use positive action over forced criticism to influence others. To follow is the *Wind & Sun Aesop Fable.*

The Wind was quarrelling with the Sun, saying that the Wind was more powerful than the Sun. They saw a man walking below and the Wind said "Let's prove who is the stronger by having a bet as to which of us would be able to make the man take his jacket off."

The Wind went first, the Sun slid behind a cloud. The Wind began blowing fiercely against the man. Yet, as the man grew colder and colder, he only wrapped himself up more snugly in his jacket, clutching at it tightly so as to keep a firm grip no matter how hard the wind might be blowing. Thus the Wind did the man no harm at all and failed to make him take off his jacket. Next, the Sun came from behind the cloud smiling. The Sun began to shine softly upon the man so brightly that the very air of the day grew hotter and hotter. The man immediately took off his jacket and threw it over his shoulder.

The Storyteller may use this Aesop fable, if the goal is to let someone know that Gentle Persuasion is stronger than force when someone doesn't want to do something.

But, to me, that fable was too esoteric for my customer base. So I took its essence and countered with the idiom "You can lead a horse to water, but you can't make him drink!" Wrong, you can make him drink. So I told the story of how I would exercise the horse. I would run the stallion around and around until he was so thirsty, he then drank of his own accord. If you want a recalcitrant person to do it your way, don't say it's my way or it's the highway; instead, make him thirsty for the results that your way will benefit him. Gentle persuasion is stronger than force.

I was challenged by a client who had thrown up his hands in despair and wouldn't believe that all he had to do was institute a few simple moves. What I was recommending for him to do was falling on deaf ears. A few days later, I walked into his office to tell him a story. Rather than repeating the laundry list of the things he needed to do, I had drafted a story that had two morals. First, always try to find a simple solution. Small action steps are better than contracting paralysis by analysis. Second, if someone is proposing a solution, listen! It matters not the age, education or the experience of the person.

Here's the Short Version of the story:

"A truck driver was racing to get home to see his son's first varsity football game and, in his reckless rush, he slammed his big rig into a tunnel beneath a train trestle. Even though there was a big yellow Height sign showing that the clearance was 11.8 feet, he gambled and lost. The truck was stuck in the entrance to the tunnel, wedged in a way that you couldn't go forward or backward. It was a square circle. Try as they may, neither the police nor the highway engineers could figure out how to remove the truck without causing great damage to the tunnel.

Time was ticking away. He already had missed the kick-off. After two hours had passed, the driver knew for sure he was going to miss his son's game. By now a crowd had gathered. When a young boy of 10 called out, "I know how to free the truck." They dismissed him with disdainful looks. How could a child know the answer when we professionals are challenged to provide a solution to this calamity?

The young boy didn't give up. His voice was heard repeatedly saying, "I know how to free the truck." Finally, the person in charge said in an annoying tone, "Ok, young man, how do you propose to free the truck?" The boy answered, "It's simple. You don't need a big solution. Just let the air out of the tires! That will lower the truck's height and free the truck." That's a great story to tell when someone is making a big deal out of something that's very simple.

Here's a true story I love to tell to make the point that you must always tell the truth when you are trying to close a prospect. Never give the impression that you're more knowledgeable than you really are. It will come back to bite you. The story I'm about to tell you is true!

My mother always wanted to be discovered by the likes of Bugs Berkley and star in one of his musical extravaganzas. That never happened, but the desire never evaporated with time. So when I came out to California to start producing films, TV commercials and sports programming, my mother came to an unfounded conclusion that now that her son was here in Hollywood, he must know where all the stars live. Wrong. The only star I knew was John Wayne and that was because our daughters played tennis together here in Newport Beach.

We had been here only nine months when the phone rang and it was my mother inviting herself to visit the grandkids. What a ploy. It was the Hollywood scene she really wanted to see. A few days after she arrived, she asked, "Will you take me to see the stars' homes in Hollywood?" Now, I have two options: I can get a map and look to see where the stars live or I can just point at the houses and say whatever name comes to mind. Seeing that at the time she was 85, I thought I could get away with pointing and fabricating. If I saw a mail box that had the name Martin on it, I would say that's where Dean Martin lives. The bigger the mansion, the bigger the star lived there. I had Rock Hudson living behind golden gates, Carol Burnett and Clark Cable living side by side. I was in full stride. Driving home she was so happy. I had made a dream come true.

That's the good news. Several weeks later, before flying back to Boston, she asked with a loving, motherly smile, "Would you take me back to see the mansions of the Stars?' Again, I had two choices. I could buy a map or do what I had done before, weave a gossamer web of deceit. I thought being 85, she couldn't possibly remember who lived in all those homes I had shown her. Wrong! She *could* remember. I couldn't. I would say that's Tony Curtis' home and she would shake her head and say "You told me that was where Fred Astaire lived." I couldn't remember. I had Tom Cruise and Sly Stallone living in the homes where I had previously said Milton Berle and Jimmy Stewart lived. I don't think I got one residence right. A great business lesson was learned. Entrepreneurs and Dreamers will always have a more passionate memory than you, so never hype them with facts you can't substantiate.

Driving home, the silence was deafening. Out of embarrassment, I had now slid beneath the steering wheel. To break the ice, I said: "I want to show you John Wayne's home." She crinkled her face with a look of *whatever*. Although I no longer had any credibility, I did know where John Wayne's house was. When I drove up and she saw how modest his home looked compared to the mansions I had just shown her in Bel Air, she shrugged in disappointment. She was right, the front of his home was average but the back was beautiful; it viewed the yachts in Newport Harbor. She skeptically said, "Ok, let's get out and you take a picture of me next to John Wayne's mailbox." As I'm getting ready to take a picture, up goes the garage door and here is John Wayne taking out a bag of garbage. He looked up and said "Fawcett, what are you doing?" I said "Duke, I'm taking a picture of my mother." Still holding the garbage bag, he went over and introduced himself. And, for more than ten minutes, they talked and I took pictures. When she flew back home, she framed the pictures of herself with John Wayne holding his garbage. Here's the motherly punch line she would tell all her sisters: "My son knows where all the stars live, except he has a very bad memory."

Storytelling draws a prospect or client into the point you're making. It's a wonderful proxy for our own experience to be relatable to the listener. Stories show us which behaviors lead to which outcomes. They have the power to move the prospect into a conversation.

Besides, you become a masterful storyteller and help your Sales Manager to create *"story-like"* testimonials that can be told by you and the sales force. Keep your ear tuned to hear about successes that can be shared in a story manner. What I have found successful for gathering storytelling materials is for you to present sample sales challenges and listen to how they would overcome. Then the trick is to take what they say and evolve it into an interest story that can be told and re-told again. It will amaze you how your best salespeople will have the best answers. That's wonderful because when he/she tells how they solved that challenge, it trains the others in attendance. From the information gathered, you create several easily-communicated stories.

When I'm on a stage lecturing and I want to make the point that working together is a necessity to grow the company, I give the audience my paper clip exercise. I begin by having everyone visualize a large paper-clip. See its shape. Now unwind that paper clip in your mind and begin to visualize what you could do with the clip. Let me give you an example. The paper clip could be used to hang a Christmas bulb. Now you have two minutes to write down all the uses you can think of. Ok? Go. You have thirty seconds left. The time is up, put down your pens. Ok, how many of you have written down 25 uses? Raise your hands. No hands will go up because is impossible to write down 25 in two minutes. How many of you have 15? Again, no hands. How about 10? One person's hand may go up. The average is 8.

Now here comes the marketing punch line: "I want each of you to read what's on your list and every time you hear a similar use, cross it off. Add any new use to your list. At the end, when we tally the total uses, we will have 25 uses; many times more uses than what we had written down. It becomes very obvious to the participants that working together is much more powerful than doing it alone. I encourage you to employ this exercise.

Why Stories Are Told:

* To share knowledge and experiences a la "The Paper Clip."

* To inspire and motivate people to understand the point you're making.
* To connect and emotionally engage with people.
* To influence people * To create faith for your vision.

When Do We Tell Stories?

We tell Stories all the time, whether it's formally or informally. The following are just a few examples of where Storytelling can be used to put octane into a presentation:

* Selling a service and/or product via the phone
* Introducing yourself/company to a new client
* Focusing a team on the goal and/or to get team buy-in
* Managing team/client relationships
* Whiteboard & PowerPoint presentations

Death by PowerPoint

In the 12th Commandment we will discuss the reasons to *Ditch PowerPoint*. Death by PowerPoint has become a common way to describe the lack of interactivity and boredom engendered by slide presentations. You have only one chance to stand out from the crowd and slides aren't the answer.

Here are two ways you or your salespeople can boost performance using "visual storytelling" instead of slides. Whether using a whiteboard, a flipchart, the back of an envelope or desktop-sharing-software, savvy salespeople are now using the visual storytelling approach to engage with prospects in a way that will set them apart from the competition:

#1: Stories Are More Lethal Than Bullets.

Your presentation should be much more than just a list of bullets; it should be a compelling, visual narrative designed to showcase your products and services and how they deliver unique value.

#2: Practice Becoming a Storyteller.

With the visual storytelling approach, it's essential that you immerse yourself in the content. Why? Because, in order to draw something, it needs to be in your head. The board isn't going to draw itself! So, pair up with a colleague and take turns presenting the material in a real-world situation. You should practice the story multiple times until you've got it down cold. First, master the visual flow and focus on the content accurately on your own. Once you've got the flow and content mastered to the point where you can draw out the entire whiteboard without referring to notes, integrate the script and practice presenting the story "in role" to your peers on an actual whiteboard. Whether you're planning to deliver your whiteboard in person or remotely, make sure you test out the presentation with an actual customer you trust. The question you want to ask is: "Does this story resonate with you?" The type of feedback you are looking for here is whether or not you are hitting the right customer challenges and *pain* points. You want to make sure your "day-in-the-life-of" story starts off with the major concerns that keep your prospects up at night.

Conclusion: I would definitely recommend that you become a member of Toastmasters. It's a fun experience that pays great sales dividends! Feedback is necessary to become an effective Storyteller and at Toastmasters you will get feedback. If you haven't the time to join, then make the time. Don't wait. The time will never be right. The best way to learn, after personal experiences, is through stories. They draw you in and provide a wonderful proxy for our own personal experience. Stories are memorable and concrete and full of emotion. Stories show us which behaviors lead to which outcomes. They have the power to move us *into* the narrative and we begin to simulate the experience. As your customer begins to mentally engage with the story, he/she moves into the role of participant and, at the same time, moves away from the role of critic.

Very few, if any MBA programs, have a course in storytelling. Storytelling acumen is where the money is. Again you're ahead of the game.

6ᵗʰ Commandment:
Thou Shall P Four More Times

In the olden, golden days you had only to concentrate on the four Ps: Product, Price, Placement and Promotion For forty years of my fifty-year career the marketing mix fell into a group of four variables:

Product: Brand Name, Word Ownership, Targeted Sales Messages, Packaging, and Servicing.

Price: Price Points, List price, Discounts, Slot Allowances and Credit Terms.

Promotion: Advertising, Sales Promotions, Trade Shows and Public Relations.

Placement: Channels, Coverage, Inventory, Transportation and Logistics.

The original 4 Ps take the seller's viewpoint of the market, not the buyer's view. The new Ps are customer-driven. With the Internet exploding onto the marketing scene, the consumer had become more educated and better informed. This new breed of buyer is more interested in relationships than just the price per se. They are interested in products and services to be immediately available. Color them green! Is it good for the environment? How are the products disposed of? Are products found on the internet?

The four (4) Ps that had been used for decades to get a client's product successfully to market became under-nourished and needed an infusion of *new school* tactics. The e-commerce dynamics of the internet totally changed the marketing landscape. It gave birth to four more Ps: Purple, Permission, Persuade, and Papoose.

Purple: The Purple P describes something phenomenal, something counter-intuitive. Its origin comes from Seth Godin's best-seller *Purple*

Cow: Cows are not distinctive; if you have seen one, you have seen them all. No one writes poems or love songs about cows. But, if among a herd of cows grazing in the green field permutated with flatulent gas, there was one PURPLE cow among the white ones, you would zone in and pay immediate attention to that purple cow. You would word-of-mouth it to others. You would Blog about it! As of today, set a goal to create clutter-cutting advertising and *Purple Cow* marketing strategies that will set your product or service apart from all others. Don't let yourself or your advertising agency fall into *mediocre*. Your advertising needs a *Purple Cow* sales message to make a person stop and give full attention to it. The market is so crowded with advertising clutter that, to be noticed, a product and its marketing need to be remarkable to be seen at all, let alone to sell.

I guarantee, when that differentiation happens, sales will significantly increase. A great example of a remarkable campaign was the challenge that a major insurance company faced when they wanted to change its name and not be lost in the herd. The Purple Cow in this case was a persistent duck. Do you know the duck? You're right it's AFLAC. I want to make it very clear that counter-intuitive differentiation does not always work but what always does work is a remarkable campaign strategy based on perceived value.

Here is my recipe that makes a campaign memorable. The item you're going to serve is a value salad. There are six secret ingredients. As I said to Caesar, "Mix it." I know it's too corny, but I couldn't resist.

- The salad has to be very simple.
- It has to be remarkable enough for a person to pay attention and try it.
- Serve it to a small group who cares. Test & Test.
- Make it easy to tell their friends. Name your Purple Cow.
- Focus on early adopters. Make your commercials appeal to the "genuine switchables".
- The salad's dressing is Italian blogging. Make them a value proposition that they can't refuse.

Permission: *Permission Marketing* allows marketers to obtain consent or permission from customers or prospects before sending them marketing messages. The phrase *Permission Marketing* was coined and popularized in 1999 by Seth Godin, former Vice President of Direct Marketing for Yahoo. *Permission Marketing* is also referred to as *Opt-in Marketing*. Opt-in occurs when an individual subscribes to receive marketing messages. Because of this, *Opt-in* carries a high response rate and produces fewer complaints. A *confirmed Opt-in* allows the marketer to send an email to the recipient to confirm that he or she has just been added to the subscription list. The individual then has the option to *unsubscribe* (or *opt-out*) immediately by replying or clicking on the link provided in the email.

It is more effective than other forms of marketing because consumers control what kinds of messages they will receive, which products and services they are interested in, and under what conditions they will perform. The most effective media for *Permission Marketing* is the internet because internet users, in particular, place more value on information (control) and are more likely to respond negatively to messages aimed only at selling. What is unique about this form of marketing is that it holds distinct advantages for both consumers and marketers.

To heighten the level of *Permission*, the marketer provides more incentives to motivate the potential customer. The *Permission* marketer then becomes someone who is trustworthy of providing a service or product. Then you leverage permission into profits.

Marketers Fail To Believe That Permission Does Expire

Permission Marketing works only if it is managed with care at every step. When consumers lose interest in your products and services, they view the prior granted permission to be obsolete and interpret future emails to be unsolicited. Therefore, in order to translate *Permission* into long-term sales, marketers must nurture that *Permission* by renewing and rewarding the *Permission*.

Permission is a state of mind and thus can be interpreted differently by consumers and marketers. In order to retain customers, marketers must adopt certain guidelines to manage relationships with their customers:

- A guaranteed way to lose a *permission-giver* is to add something extra without getting permission. For example: "If a customer gives you permission to do 'A' and you then add in 'B,' in many cases it wipes away the permission for "A." Keep in mind that you run a risk by adding another permission to the original.

- Most consumers are unwilling to give permission because of privacy issues but, when they do, they expect to be served with trust and respect for their privacy. It's very important that you provide your customers with a link to your privacy policy. It gives them a sense of dealing with a legitimate source. Give customers options and allow them to have confidence that you will honor their requests. Tell them outright that you won't distribute or sell your private information. Although this seems like an obvious marketing "no-no," many businesses fail to see that and, as a result, the trust is broken by such practices.

- Reinforce your relationship with customers by reminding them how they were included on your list. A simple statement in the introduction to your email can serve this purpose.

* Don't waste time and money sending emails to big lists. Do it right. Unlike *Permission Marketing*, spam is generally unwanted and often perceived as an infringement of privacy, in addition to being ignored and/or deleted by the recipient most of the time.

* It's of paramount importance that you immediately put into place a system with a dedicated person to test, track and evaluate your permission email marketing campaigns in real-time, giving you immediate feedback.

Don't sell until you have established a relationship with the consumer. Be patient. Provide free valuable information. My guideline is a ratio of three-to-one. The customer receives three electronic packets of free information before I make one sales solicitation. I then have a follow-up rule of two emails. If there's no positive sales response, don't waste time, cut them loose.

Persuade: *Persuasion* is diplomacy at its best. It's the ability to convince potential customers to accept your idea or buy your product. Why do you say *Persuasion* is a new P? Today's persuasion is in tandem with patience. You can't just start the selling syllogism and pitching your product right off the bat. If you do, the new breed of consumers won't listen! You need to create a conversation with the potential client.

You need to build a relationship and that takes patience. This was hard lesson for me to learn because I was taught the ABCs of selling: **A**lways, **B**e **C**losing from the moment the client is within hearing distance. That is no longer the way to sell. The sales technique in today's market is patient *Persuasion*.

Donald Trump insists, "You don't want to force a person to accept your ideas. That's a recipe for disaster. Your objective should be to make your adversaries feel like they are your partner, not a victim. In successful negotiations all parties should feel satisfied with the outcome."

You'll persuade people if you negotiate with civility. Walk in their shoes. Understand what they want and what you believe they will buy or sell for. One of the courses at the Harvard Business School I enjoyed the most was the Art of Negotiating. One point the professor kept hammering home was, before you enter into the room to negotiate, you must have determined what your *Walk Away Price* is going to be. If it goes below that price, you walk mentally. Someone wants to pay too little or you don't want to pay any more then you know when to walk. Negotiating takes place in the delta of the offering price and the *Walk Away Price*. But don't be the first to physically leave the negotiation table. Make your final offer or acceptance and just smile and sit. It's never over until the other party walks away!

Most deadlocks seem to concern money, but there are usually other elements that can be adjusted to make an agreement possible. If you concentrate on solving the problem rather than on defeating your opponent, the variables can often be re-packaged in a way that will meet the needs of both parties. See Commandment #16 (Negotiating With Your Ears).

Papoose: I coined the phrase "*Papoose Marketing*" because it clearly describes Affiliate Marketing in that it conveys the image that someone is carrying you on their marketing back. Affiliate marketing uses one website to drive traffic to another. It's a form of online marketing which is frequently overlooked by advertisers. While search engines, e-mail, and website syndication capture much of the attention of online retailers, "*Affiliate Papoose Marketing*" carries a much lower profile. Still, affiliates continue to play a significant role in e-retailers' marketing strategies. Where it plays a major role is in the Google Ranking Triad. N.B. It takes into consideration for optimization the affiliate traffic that is driven to your website. (See Commandment # 2)

Papoose Marketing is one the few business endeavors where everyone involved is working for success. The advertiser wants you to succeed and your affiliate network is cheering you on. They only succeed if you do.

Cost per action/sale methods require that referred visitors do more than visit the advertiser's website before the affiliate receives a commission. The advertiser must convert that visitor first. It is in the best interest for the affiliate to send the most closely-targeted traffic to the advertiser as possible to increase the chance of a conversion. The risk and loss is shared between the affiliate and the advertiser.

JV Affiliate Marketing Math

Let's say your website has a value of $1 and a sales conversion rate of 1%. You might decide that you'd be willing to pay 25% of the sales price. If the price were $100 you would pay the affiliate $25 for sending you a customer. The next step is to find a JV Affiliate Partner.

* Using an affiliate network like Tribalfusio.com will speed up the process of finding a site for your advertising. This site provides guidance and third-party resources for creative ad design as well.
* Another excellent affiliate site is Adbrite.com. Their claim-to-fame is 290 million impressions every day on more than 100,000 sites.
* Quantcast.com is a site dedicated to internet demographics, which is precisely what you need, a clarification of your target-market.

The potential Affiliate JV Partner will ask you two questions:

(1) What's your value per customer? and (2) What's your conversion rate?

You already know that that every visitor who visits your website is worth $1 and you know that your current conversion rate is 1%. Therefore, it is generally a safe assumption that the visitors he sends will convert at the same rate as your other visitors.

If the JV Affiliate has a list of ten thousand leads, you would pay him $.25 for every lead he sent to your landing page. If the conversion rate of 1% stayed constant, it would be worth $2,500 to him and $7,500 to you. If his list is larger, the numbers grow accordingly.

What if you had an opt-in conversion rate of 5%. If 10% of those who had opted-in eventually bought your product, you have increased your overall sales conversion by fifty percent to 1.5%.

Merchants favor affiliate marketing because in most cases it uses a "pay for performance" model, meaning that the merchant does not incur a marketing expense unless results are accrued (excluding any initial setup cost). Some businesses owe much of their success to this marketing technique, a notable example being Amazon.com.

Conclusion:

Internet marketing is easy. Find a **P**urple Cow, put a **P**apoose on its back, **P**ersuade her to give you **P**ermission to have affiliates milk her. Those new four Ps (Purple Cow, Persuasion, Permission and Papoose) are now merged with the original four: Price, Product, Promotions and Placement. Result: You will have established the base to build your marketing-mix platform. I don't know the key to super success, but I do know the key to failure is not P-ing eight times.

Hawthorne Direct Infomercial Rating Guide

CAT. A	STRONG (5 Points)	GOOD (3 Points)	FAIR (1 Point)	SCORE Rating
1.	A celebrity endorsement	A charismatic personality (+1)	TV pitchman talent	
2.	Product has 5 to 1 markup	Mark-up less than 5 to 1 but more than 3 to 1	Mark-up 3 to 1 or less	
3.	Product has high ad allowable	Medium ad allowable	Low ad allowable	
4.	Price $59.95 or less or lead generator	Payment plan switch or positive	$149 or more negative cash flow	
5.	Good upsell or backend potential	Good premium or offer switch	Limited upsell or backend potential	
6.	Existing merchants credit card	Will be able to obtain card	Difficult to obtain	
CAT. B	STRONG (3 Points)	GOOD (2 Points)	FAIR (1 Point)	SCORE Rating
7.	Product has existing testimonials	Testimonials can be paid for	No testimonials are available	
8.	Full 100% money-back guarantee	Limited or conditional guarantee	Vague	
9.	Product has proven retail or direct sales	There is similar successful product	Product acceptance not yet clear	
10.	Product has blue-collar appeal	Products appeal to educated consumer	Product appeals to very upscale consumer	
11.	Ratio of value to price very attractive	Value good, but price relatively high	Perceived value low, price high	
12.	Product easily demonstrated (kitchen gadget, etc.)	Can't be fully demonstrated (success item, audiotapes)	Can't be demonstrated at all	
13.	Product fulfills a dream, makes life easier	Has solid perceived value	Hard to understand the value	
14.	Product is life-supporting	Product works	Questionable product	
15.	Product makes excellent 60 second commercial	Questionable spot results	Best in print media only	

Total Rating Points:

For Fawcett to consider to produce or invest the rating must be between 46 – 57
Fawcett Productions 36 Via Barcaza, Coto de Caza, CA 92679

7th Commandment: Thou Shall keep The Five Secrets to Stardom

William Shatner
Pierce Brosnan
John Wayne
Dick Van Dyke
Orson Wells
Jane Fonda
Dean Martin
Dr. Laura
Jerry Lewis
Arthur Ashe
Bobby Riggs
Robin Leach
Dinah Shore
Sidney Poitier
Ricardo Montalban
Quincy Jones
Debbie Reynolds
Florence Henderson
Terry Bradshaw
Mr T

Over the years, I have had the opportunity to work with a cavalcade of stars. We all know the value of celebrity endorsements when it comes to producing infomercials and Direct-Response TV commercials. If you ink the right pitch person who identifies with your target market, you're on your way to buying a wheelbarrow to take home the money. Tony Little built a three billion dollar empire hawking his products on TV. Bio Slim grossed eighty million dollars in its first year. Prolong lubricant went from a zero share of market and five-hundred thousand dollars in debt to grossing thirty-five million dollars. Sham Wow, Magic Jack and Snuggie are all multi-million dollar income-producers. Say George Foreman and up comes the word grill. Say Tiger Woods and one of Nike's products comes to mind. But before you go looking for a spokesperson, you need to know if your product or service has the business characteristics to be successful. To that end, let me tell you what I require my clients to do first:

Every month Fawcett Productions receives inquiries asking me if I think their product would be suitable for a successful infomercial. The answer to the question is, I don't know if it will be successful. But I can, with certainty, tell the person if it will *not* be successful. Because I hate to tell someone that their baby isn't pretty, I have them fill-in the "Infomercial Rating Guide" (seen on the opposite page). If they don't accumulate at least forty-six rating points, in my professional opinion, it would be a waste of their money to produce an Infomercial and buy media time.

Instructions: Category A points range from 5 to 1. In Category B the points range from 3 to 1. The term "ad allowable" means what percentage of the product's selling price are you willing to allocate to buy media. As a rule, your "cost of goods" should not exceed 20% of the selling price. You must be aware that if you offer a payment plan you will probably be in a negative cash position for the first two monthly payments. For example, let's say the selling price is $99 and you are offering three payments of $33; Cost of Goods 20%; Advertising/telemarketing 55%; totals 75%. That means it's not until the third month that you have a positive cash flow.

Please understand, I'm not implying that installment plans are bad. That's far from the truth. I'm just making you aware of the cash requirements that are associated with monthly payment plans. What I recommend is a two-step goal. The first goal is to get the viewer to try the product for a one-time special introductory price. The second step is to immediately get them on a monthly continuity program with automatic shipping. (The rating evaluation process can be filled-in on my site at: *www.FawcettInfomercials.com*).

If it's a go, then the next step is to follow my 5 Secrets to Stardom.

The first secret is to choose a celebrity that the public can identify with your product or service. It's best when the buying public has prior knowledge of the relationship. Just to have a celebrity endorsement is a waste of money if there is no real relationship with the product. To further explain the importance of having a recognizable relationship, let me share a few examples with you. My client, City of Hope, one of most prestigious cancer treatment centers in the world contracted me to produce a fund-raising Infomercial. I chose Pierce Brosnan to be its spokesperson. The relationship here was that the public knew his wife had died of breast cancer. The audience immediately identified with his compassionate message. The board members were excited to be using the power of television to generate donations, but they were very concerned about the cost of the in-bound 800 number and the collection process. To eliminate those concerns, I spent two months negotiating with major phone companies to allow the call-in donations to be billed to a 900 number, thereby eliminating the high cost of having to use an 800 call-in number. And more importantly, there were no collection problems because the donations were billed to the donor's telephone bill. Although the Infomercial won the prestigious Jordan Whitney Award for the best infomercial and the Aurora Award for video excellence, the real winner was the City of Hope.

Here's another example of relationship endorsement: A major home security company wanted us to produce a 60-second DRTV commercial for a very inexpensive door lock security system that looked like a coat-hanger bent into a figure eight. Although it worked, it just looked too simple for a person to pay $19.95 for it. To enhance the product's visual creditability I hired Mr.T, who had gained fame early in his career by winning the Bouncer of the Year Award. One of the competitive challenges he faced was to crash though a series of barroom doors. The intercity audience knew about his achievement. In the studio we built and bolted down two similar exterior door settings. The first door represented the average person's door. The other door was similar but it had the company's *Loop-Lock* mounted to its casing. I called out "action." Mr. T ran at the door, not only did he bust in, he smashed the door to smithereens. I was stunned. Immediately, fear ran through my mind because we only had a one-take budget. What if the *Loop-Lock* didn't hold and this door was also smashed? The good news is the security device held and the product went on to be a successful smash hit.

On the other hand, if the celebrity you choose has no imaginable relationship to the product, expect the worst! A great example of this faux pas was when Turkish Airlines hired Kobe Bryant to be their spokesperson. Kobe has never flown Turkish Airlines, nor has he ever been to Turkey and is not planning on going. Bryant's agent said: "Kobe is a recognized global ambassador for peace so it works." The Armenian population in the United States fervently disagreed because of the past genocide.

It's continually an uphill battle for Sears, Wal-Mart, Kohls and Target to transform their image into a fashion store for young shoppers. To accomplish that image transformation they hire teen queens. Wal-Mart has Miley Cyrus. Britney Spears is the spokesperson for Kohl's fashion line. What's interesting is their fans know that Miley and Britney probably don't shop in these stores for their clothes, yet it doesn't matter. It's a very expensive, "top-of-the-mind" marketing strategy that hasn't as yet changed the fashion image of these stores.

In certain rare circumstances you might want to get a celebrity who is the antithesis of the identification with the product. The absurd contrast immediately gets the viewer's attention. A good example: many years ago in the late 70's, when tennis was the rage and everyone was playing, I produced and directed a featured film tennis documentary. Who did I choose to open the film? John Wayne. No one could ever visualize John Wayne in a tennis outfit and he never was. The trick to making this contrast endorsement work is to provide a visual point why John Wayne was selected. In this case we named the film Shotgun Sunday. The opening scene was a montage of tennis elites firing off serves to the sounds of gunfire. When the firing stopped, John Wayne walked into the scene and said something along the lines of, "The Ok Corral of tennis takes place Sunday at high noon at Wimbledon. Let the battle begin!" My tennis film was nominated for a Cannes Film Festival Documentary Award.

Endorsements don't work unless they are age and interest-specific. For example: Cher, Michael Jordan, Jack Nicholas and Paul McCartney are relevant to the fifty-plus market, as Kobe Bryant, Tiger Woods and Madonna are meaningful endorsers for the forty plus market. The eighteen to twenty year-olds would be most influenced with an extreme sports star or the latest rocker like Usher or Lady Gaga. Plus, the Y generation is looking for authentic, trusted advice from young, contemporary entrepreneurs like Mark Zuckerberg, Larry Parks and Bill Gates. They find hyperbola offensive and a sales turn-off. What I'm stressing is for endorsements to be effective, they must be age and interest-specific.

The second endorsement secret is to create your own spokesperson. Be your own TV star maker. Before Billy Mays, Vince with Sammy Wow, Richard Simmons, the Juice man, were TV pitch people; they were just ordinary people with extraordinary sales charisma. One of the primary benefits for creating your own charismatic spokesperson is that you're in complete control. It's much more affordable than paying those outrageous celebrity endorsement fees. Plus, you're not held hostage by the celebrity's agent. Where do I begin the search for my spokesperson? You go to county fairs and watch the gizmo pitch people. Check out local stage production companies. Go to the local comedy club. When the budget allows, I suggest you consider going to a casting-call agency and have them round up the talent for you. You'll be surprised how quickly you'll discover a person who will be an ideal spokesperson for your product.

The third secret for DRTV success is for you to make empirical, not emotional, decisions. Base them on cold, hard, timely facts. To ensure your success, you must conduct a focus group. Here's a low-cost tip you can do yourself. Conduct two eyeball-to-eyeball focus groups with eleven people in each group. The first focus group will give you intellectual insights as to what you need to ask the second group. The secret here is to make the changes that the first group suggested and inculcate them into your second presentation. I usually pay the participants $60 for a two-hour focus group ($60 x 22= $1,300 + $250 in small space ads = $1,550 (US). Please understand, I'm not saying in any way that the companies that conduct behavioral research are not of value. The opposite is true. But, if you have a limited budget, I have found my two groups of eleven each will produce incredible findings.

It's not what you think is important; it's what your customer thinks is important. I've seen it too many times where the small business owner is not objective. They blindly fall in love with the product and/or the spokesperson. Once you have tested the commercial, it's show time. When the curtain goes up for a 30-minute infomercial, it should work the first time and every time thereafter. If it doesn't work, even in the right hands, results can always be improved, but not usually enough to resuscitate a program that's dead on arrival. The DRTV 60-second (short-form) commercial success takes longer to determine because it's based on the times the commercial airs and is seen. Frequency begets Reach. Frequency is the benefit of success, not the key to success.

An expert direct-marketing agency will help you run a successful Infomercial campaign, but just as important is that they advise you to stop throwing your advertising dollars away if the results are not there. My advice is to make sure you choose an experienced production company that has created winners like Hawthorne Direct, Script to Screen, Thane International and of course the king, Guthy-Renker. If you have a modest production budget, I submit you should call Fawcett Infomercials. (sorry for the commercial plug).

The fourth secret lies in you understanding that direct-response is an interwoven science. You must treat DRTV and the Internet as a single channel. The Internet adds dimension to DRTV and DRTV adds scale to the internet. Your website and your DRTV commercials must be in tandem with each other. You can and must have the same copy and sales points. In both cases, your copy should be simple. Never say what you are thinking and never say what you are showing. Most importantly, make sure your storyboard runs by itself, without training wheels. Ask yourself: has the commercial entertained? Has it been informative? Would you buy the product after you saw the commercial or visited the website?

Guthy-Renker has become a dominate force by reducing its dependence on high MERs. What's an MER? It is a measurement of media efficiency. The ratio represents gross direct sales for every ad dollar spent. If, for every dollar spent, you received $2 in revenue, you would have a 2 to 1 ratio. It's very one-dimensional in that a MER measures the media efficiency for the specific commercial that just aired and doesn't take into consideration the long-term customer value. Only one out of every twenty-nine DRTV commercials actually achieves a MER ratio that would qualify as a positive ROI. If that's the case, you will want to shift your thinking to consumable products with long-term revenue streams. Instead of a one-time sale, you are looking for repeat business. Now the ratio makes economic sense!

The infomercial is an excellent way to build a brand. Many brand-building companies believe that an infomercial is a better, more-affordable media expenditure to educate the public. Thirty seconds of brand exposure to thirty minutes of product information, plus a call-to-action. In that brand-building scenario, the company is not concerned with the MER; it becomes a traditional advertising awareness campaign in their minds.

The fifth secret is creating *Urgency.* You need to create a *You Need It Now* mental state of mind. You do that by either selling the pain or selling the solution. The pain approach identifies with what the prospect is feeling. You dramatize the pain!

The sixth secret is no matter what product you are selling, my advice to my clients has always been to tap into a prospects' inner mind, where 90% of purchase decisions are made. I coined the phase *Psyche-selling*. Don't sell the product per se; sell the psychology behind the product. Mary Kay didn't sell cosmetics; she sold self-esteem. Richard Simons didn't just sell weight loss; he too sold self-esteem. An example of automotive psyche-selling: "You look like the Million Dollar Man in that Porsche." When the product has been computer software, I had them sell Pain! (Relief comes with buying my software).

Does The Name Edison Ring A Bell?

A successful DRTV campaign is like a three-legged stool. You need all three legs; otherwise it will wobble. First, you need a valuable offer. Second, you must have a media buy that matches your customer demographics. The third leg is a call-center that has experienced personnel. The reason why I drafted this sample telephone script is to provide a format for those entrepreneurs who want their staff to answer the bell because of the technical nature of their product.

(Open by establishing the purpose).
Thank you for calling _____to place an ___order.
(Introduce yourself . . . easier to get information)
My name is _____. May I have your first name?

(Call the customer by their first name)
_____, may I have your last name?

(To create professionalism ask for spelling)
How is that spelled ____?

(Call the customer by their first name)
____, may I have the phone number you're calling from?
Area code first.

(Introduction of an up-sell . . . 20% will buy)
For ordering today we have two specials _____.
Limited Time offer____. Not sold in stores. That's a savings of____.
You're going to be pleased for adding that item to your order.
(Professional Call-Centers are masters at up-sale selling)

(If a product question is asked, be brief)
__Insert your company name __is so sure you're going to _____
it's offering a money-back guarantee. You have nothing to
lose _____.

(First name again . . . preemptive approach control the call)
_____, I need the mailing address you want your product shipped to.
What credit card will you be using today? _____.
What's the account number on your card? _____.
(Once the number is given . . . repeat the number)

What's the expiration date? _____ There is a security code number that
appears on your name card. Please tell me what that number is.

(Call by first name . . . put a smile in your voice)
_____, your shipment should arrive within two weeks.

Thank you for ordering _____. Enjoy the product.

The bottom-line: If you're going to air Direct-Response TV and
Radio commercials, you need to hire a professional "call-center." It
will be money well-spent. Even if you have produced a persuasive
commercial and the media buy was excellent, everything can be lost
if you don't have a solid call-center that can close the deal and up-sell.
A call-center's role is to close warm leads, whereas telemarketing has
many roles to fulfill. Telemarketing disciplines range from identifying
and contacting prospects, contacting present customers, announcing
events and introducing new product launches.

Telemarketing Guiding Principles:
Too many business owners see telemarketing as a separate activity
from their other marketing strategies. This is a big mistake because
experience has shown me time and time again that the whole is much
greater than the sum of the parts when all the different strands to a
marketing strategy are pulling together. Your marketing strategy has
one purpose and one purpose alone: to make you money. To do that
most effectively, it all has to be going the same way. I would like to
share some helpful telemarketing tips with you:

1. Follow-up your mailing with a phone call. One of the mainstays of effective marketing is direct mail. But what isn't generally known is if you follow-up a mailing with a telephone call, you can improve results by 50 to 300 % (yes, 300%—that's not a misprint).

   If you then get the prospective customer on the phone—and we're not talking about the hard sell here—you're reminding them about the mailing they had received. Basically, the mailing softens them up for the call.

   If you're unsure how your customers will react to being sold to on the phone, don't sell to them. Selling on the phone can be tricky. You can never be quite sure what your prospect is doing when you call, so even the lightest touch with the softest intent can come at exactly the wrong moment. That's why it's important to make your approach as unobtrusive as you can. If you really are not sure how your prospects, customers and clients will react to being given a sales pitch on the phone, no matter how gentle, don't do it. Instead, use the telephone call to ask questions, gather information and ensure their needs are being met. Everyone likes to feel important and everyone likes to feel someone cares. Make no mistake, even if you call someone to just make sure they are OK, then they'll appreciate it.

   In fact, a very powerful way of up-selling your customers and clients, and for getting referrals is to call after you've made a sale, just to make sure things are satisfactory and the customer is happy.

2. I'm a big believer is writing and using scripts to make sure whatever is being said has all the right sales buttons. When a salesperson wings it, the effectiveness is reduced 60%. Use scripts, but also be flexible. Telemarketing scripts are useful, especially at the beginning of a call, because they set the entire frame of the conversation.

3. DON'T LET THE TELEMARKETER READ THE SCRIPT TO THE PROSPECT!

   That's the worst faux pas a telemarketer can make. If it sounds like it's being read, you're dead. Before you allow them to get on the phone and represent your company, make sure they have been trained so it sounds conversational. Encourage them to put their personality into the script and put a smile into their voice. Allocate time to train them. It's a wise investment. This holds true for call-centers. They must train their people to your satisfaction. *Practice makes Perfect.*

Effective communication is a process:

Consumers respond to advertising that helps them make smart purchase decisions. In research, consumers complained about the lack of information at retail stores. They laugh at the idea that traditional advertising helps them make purchasing decisions. While the Web offers a wealth of information, it doesn't offer effective demonstrations of how your product impacts their lives. Infomercials succeed by offering consumers communication demonstrations that make products meaningful. Traditional advertising usually limits itself to a single big idea or mere lifestyle messages. By contrast, infomercials persuade consumers through a communication process moving them from initial awareness to purchase. A long-form program does this by layering a set of core messages so that each undercovers a deeper understanding of the product.

YouTube is the Internet Phenomenon

YouTube is definitely not your father's method of sharing video footage. In today's age of search optimization and search engine marketing, you must be present in both worlds to gain the exposure and presence that you desire. You do that by adding the YouTube video to your website. This way you get indexed on YouTube for the video and on your website for the video, driving even more consumer interest in your direction. Video marketing is the future of marketing. It's of paramount importance that you spend time learning how to harness the power of YouTube for small business applications.

Conclusion: You must treat DRTV and the Internet as a single channel. It has become a science. It's interwoven with all aspects of social media and mobile marketing. I would caution Marketers not to invest huge chunks of their budgets into social media; there is no question that the community-building power of Facebook, Twitter and YouTube is awesome, but it's not yet measurable. Nor has it been proven that those social platforms build brands, whereas DRTV has already been proven: Snuggie, anyone? How about Shake Weight? Tae Bo & Carleton Sheets make you healthy and wealthy? or Tailgate with a George Foreman Grill?

I would be remiss not to mention Billy Mays, Billy Blanks, Richard Simmons Ron Popeil and Jack LaLanne. These pitch-legends and a galaxy of other spokespeople have sold millions and millions of dollars worth of products and services My favorite, without a doubt, is Proactive Solutions. This product was a game changer and has grown into an incredibly successful business for Guthy-Renker. A successful DRTV campaign is like a three-legged stool. You need all three legs; otherwise it will wobble: 1. A valuable offer. 2. A media buy that matches your customer demographics 3. A call-center that has experienced personnel. For the last decade *As Seen on TV* was the retail buzz word. Because of the Internet, it's being replaced with *As Seen Everywhere.*

I encourage you to become a YouTube business broadcaster. Learn all you can. Video has overtaken print; it's now the most cost-efficient way of driving traffic to your site. YouTube is a bitch that never sleeps! From a marketing standpoint, a viral YouTube video can catapult you from garage to boardroom faster than a MBA.

8th Commandment:
Thou Shall Not Sell "Texaco Milk"

Texaco-Milk? Gag me! Although that's an extreme hypothetical line extension, it's a great yellow caution light that says *slow down and think hard* before you link your core brand name with a new product. Line extensions very rarely work, yet companies continue to pump them out. Here are some stupid examples: Heinz Ketchup introduced Heinz Baby Food. Bic Lighter added Bic Pantyhose. How do these connect? Are Bic Pantyhouse for only hot chicks? Pierre Cardin Clothing now has a wine. Not to be outdone, Ed Hardy, vintage tattoo artist, has just introduced a tequila.

In a narrow sense, line extension involves taking the brand name of a successful product and attaching it to a new product you plan to introduce. Sometimes it sounds logical to add another product line. For example, A-1 Steak Sauce rationalized, because people are switching from beef to chicken, let's introduce an A-1 Poultry Sauce. Sounds good in theory but, in actuality, customers were uncomfortable saying "Pass me the A-1 Sauce for my chicken." It didn't sound right and failed.

Perdue Farms' excursion into selling frozen turkey is also a good example. Here's a brand known for *"freshness."* Suddenly, after twenty years of T.V. touting the virtues of *"freshness"*, they have abandoned it's core values and now they are selling Perdue's *"frozen"* turkey. That's right, *"frozen."* When a company departs from what they are known for, failure follows. Trust me, even if the *"frozen"* turkey advertising is well crafted, it will ring false. Plus, it dilutes the flagship brand's image

My grey-hair advice is to be very careful about considering adding a line extension. A great many things have changed in marketing in the last fifty years, but one thing that hasn't changed is executive-rushing into adding more new product lines. It sounds cool, but just be aware that there is a strong undertow.

Why does top management believe that line extension works in spite of the overwhelming evidence to the contrary? One reason is that while line extension is a loser in the long term, it generates PR, stocks show movement and it creates a new revenue stream. The Law of Perspective Management is also blinded by an intense loyalty to the company. Why else would PepsiCo have introduced Crystal Pepsi in spite of the failures of Pepsi Light and Pepsi AM?

The introduction of Coors Light caused the collapse of Coors Regular, which today sells one-fourth of what it used to. Even the King is down. After annual sales increases stretching back to the end of Prohibition, Budweiser has been slipping the last three years in a row. The cause? Bud Light.

Once successful, there will be the temptation to expand the core business' profits by adding a line extension. In spite of evidence that line extensions don't work, companies continually break the commandment and introduce new products. If you're going to enter that arena you must do four things:

#1. Make sure your new extension is more than a fad. Beware, just because a host of companies rush into a market doesn't mean it's not a fad. A good example is the Tequila market. All of sudden Tequila became the fashionable drink. Patron's sales skyrocketed and with it came a flood of new Tequila brands. The new entries' differential was focused on exquisite bottle designs, one more attractive than the other; celebrity endorsements and expensive "sipping brands." Is this a fad? Is it worthy of a line extension? I don't know. But seeing I had been in the importing and marketing of Drambuie and other cordials, if I were still in the liquor industry I would have probably considered entering the Tequila market because I already had distribution channels set in place. But if I were in another industry, as I am now, I would never have committed to a line extension. The marketing of Spirits and Cordials is, by nature, a fad industry.

#2. You need to research and determine what impact the new line will have on your present _customer base_. St John Knits manufactures and markets high-end dresses and fashion ware. The line is very appealing and flattering to the middle-age woman's figure. The company made a line-extension decision to introduce a younger design line at a more affordable price. I would presume that the decision was driven by added profits, with little regard to what the reaction of their *core* customers would be. The inevitable happened, core-customer sales dropped significantly. The lower price and the company's emphasis of this younger market had a deleterious impact; it was no longer prestigious to buy. Also it implied that the quality was less. After nine months, they discontinued that line extension. Don't make the same mistake. Your loyal customers should be your number one priority.

#3. Before you launch a new product, it's of paramount importance that you know where in the "life cycle" you'll be entering. I cringe when I hear a *profit-enamored* marketer say, "It doesn't matter at what stage in the "life cycle" you enter the market." WRONG! It's hard enough going against an established company, but entering at the end of the competitor's life cycle is almost suicidal. Life Cycles usually have four broad phases: Entry, Growth, Maturity and Decline. Conventional wisdom holds that a company should avoid entering a market in the Maturity or Decline Life Cycle phases.

The Maturity stage is fraught with expansion temptations. It's a very appealing phase. The market is proven, people are buying a similar product and you're convinced that your product is so much better that you'll capture a respectable share of the market. If you want to capture a share of market in the Maturity Cycle, then you must be able to claim a *First* in the marketplace. For example, You're the *First* to offer Home Delivery. When you take on two or three leaders who have already built substantial customer loyalty, the odds of success are indeed low, but the rewards of a simple, strategic victory are high if you go after the switchable customers. *Switchables* are those who are sufficiently unhappy with their current supplier and would be interested in being courted.

Acquisition costs for *Switchables* can be 1/5 to 1/10 of what it costs to win over a competitor's loyal customers. It's of paramount importance that you differentiate very clearly between "garage-sale" *Switchables*, who always go to the cheapest source, and "genuine" *Switchables*, who are legitimately unhappy with their current suppliers. Chronic switchers are not "investment-grade customers" and, therefore, are not worthy of long-term attention. "Genuine" *Switchables*, however, are loyal customers in play.

Where do you find "genuine" Switchables? Find out if the word is out on the street that your competitors' customers are receiving poor service. Listen to learn if there is a growing mismatch between what their customers want and what is being offered. Other green light opportunities: post-merger confusion and financial uncertainty.

Caution: Acquiring competitors' most loyal customers can be prohibitively expensive, but identifying and attracting their switchable customers, those who are sufficiently unhappy with their current supplier and welcome being courted, can be extremely attractive. Companies need to differentiate very clearly between chronic "garage-sale" switchers and "genuine" *Switchables*.

#4. Don't for one minute think that the small business owner isn't faced with similar expansion temptations, but this time it's not called line extensions. It's now called SKUs. As the great philosopher, Mr. T, would say: "I pity the fool who has too many SKUs to sell." Where is it written that the more you have to sell, the more you will sell? The more SKUs (Stock Keeping Units) your competitors have, the better your chances are to succeed. Don't fall into the booby trap that "more is better." It's a proven fact that the more SKUs and line extensions you have to sell, the more difficult it is to concentrate on the few products that generate 80% of your bottom-line profit.

Along with cutting down on the number of SKUs you sell, cut loose those customers who require a great deal of customer service and contribute very little revenue and the better off you'll be. You will now be able to service bigger revenue-generating customers even better.

How do you know what customers to cut loose? My wife of forty-nine years has an innovative way of knowing what she should cut loose from her closets and give to Goodwill. It works this way. Every time she wears a particular outfit she hangs the item in a different direction in the closet. What she hasn't worn from Fall to Winter she packs it up and off it goes to Goodwill. It holds true for the items she doesn't wear during Spring thru Summer. Of course, there are exceptions to that rule. In your business closet there are low-revenue customers who require a greater deal of service and require a multitude of special SKUs. It's a new season. Rid yourself of that demanding business wardrobe.

Conclusion: Don't sell Texaco-Milk. Be double cautious when you're contemplating the introduction of a line-extension. As we discussed in Commandment #1, for a new brand to succeed, it ought to be *First* in a new category. Or, the new brand ought to be positioned as an alternative to the leader. An excellent example was when Budweiser created the category of Light Beer. They positioned themselves as number #1 in Light Beers.

Before you jump into a "hot" market, along with a flood of other companies, make sure it's not a fad. Check out the research. Analyze what would cause customers to give up on the product. The main exodus would be if the product didn't work and/or it was a sham. There was a company called Power Balance that had created this year's version of the copper bracelet; it was advertised as being embedded with a frequency that allegedly improves the body's energy flow. The Power Balance wristband was worn by Shaq, Alex Rodriquez, Teemu Selanne, David Beckham and sales zoomed. They sold three million units. When, in 2010, they wanted to launch their energy wristband in Australia, the government required them to prove that their product worked. The partners came forward, smiled and said: "We have no proof." But it was a very profitable placebo. Don't be a sheep and follow others; have others follow you!

Make sure you know the "life cycle" phase your competitors are in and where in the life cycle your product will be introduced. Lastly, size doesn't matter (that will be a comfort to most men); little is more. Decease your SKUs and cut your non-revenue-generating clients and you'll increase your profitability. Many times the number of SKUs in your warehouse is in direct relationship to whether or not you post a profit.

If you do launch a new product line, focus your attention on the big three:

1. Switchables Customers who are dissatisfied with your competitors' service or products.
2. *High-Profit Customers* who would generate the most revenue. Limit your solicitation to low-revenue-producing customers.

3. *Long-Term-Growth Customers* who are important because the introduction of a new SKU or line extension will probably not be profitable in the short term and, therefore, you will need long-term customers to turn a positive cash flow.

By far, the most violated law in this book is the Law of Line Extension. When a company becomes incredibly successful, it invariably plants the seeds for expansion. More SKUs to please more customers is a very dangerous mindset. When you try to be all things to all people, you inevitably wind up in trouble. "I'd rather be strong somewhere than weak everywhere."

9th Commandment:
Thou Shall Be A "First Impression" Junky

My relationship Geiger Counter ticks loudest on first impressions! It's amazing how quickly we decide whether we like or dislike a person. But that decision is secondary to finding out where that person is mentally coming from. To me first impressions are a preview of coming attractions. I have listed below some of the most common greet and meet impressions that I have encountered:

> I'm superior, you're not!
> Big egos, little ears find themselves fascinating.
> Seems to shows interest, doesn't take interest.
> It's my way or the perfectionist's highway.
> Not in the moment, mind elsewhere.
> Perseverance is my middle name.
> Rejoice is a choice mindset.
> He or she is in the reinvention stage.
> There are many more . . .

In this example I have chosen six celebrities who I have worked with. Nice guys all, but all so different with their meet and greets.

What do Orson Wells, John Wayne, Dick Van Dyke, Rodney Dangerfield Arthur Ashe, Frank Sinatra and William Shatner have in common? The answer is NOTHING!

Nothing when it comes to meeting people and leaving a long lasting first impression. It's very difficult to overcome a first Impression. Orson Wells' greeting was one of "I'm intellectually superior and you are not." John Wayne was one of "Show me what you've got, pilgrim." Ricardo

Montalban's public persona was the same as his real life, a very loving man. Dick Van Dyke's first impression was of one who wants you to have fun. Rodney Dangerfield lived his persona on and off the stage. He was never in the moment with you. When you met Arthur Ashe, you knew he was man who wanted to help mankind. He had time for you.

Let's start with Orson Wells. I was very excited knowing that I was going to meet and film Hollywood legend Orson Wells, the genius who directed the movie "*Citizen Kane*,"

a movie that has been acclaimed to be one the greatest movies of all time. This was the man who created the radio drama, *War of the Worlds,* that had people believing that there was an invasion by aliens. Panic broke out. Then, a few days later, he turned around and said it was just a prank. People didn't think it was funny. Lesson: Audiences don't like to be misled. A more contemporary example of being misled is the finale of the successful television show, *Lost*. The shows' creators told us that all of those mysteries we were trying to unravel in the preceding five seasons would not be answered. In their minds, it shouldn't matter. First-class betrayal. Bottom line: never mislead a customer or an investor because it will never be forgotten and news about "misleading" travels faster than good deeds.

I knew going in that Orson would be difficult to deal with, but I didn't know how difficult! The documentary I was directing was about Orson's close friend, Frank Lloyd Wright, one of the world's greatest architects. The story centered around how his Taliesin disciples were carrying on since their maestro's death. After I introduced myself, he never looked up. I stood there for what seemed like an hour and then he looked up and greeted me with: "What is the etymology of the word Taliesin?"

All my life business life I have lived the essence of Commandment #16 Be prepared, know what challenging questions you'll be asked. Remember negotiations are won before you ever negotiate. My answer was: "The word Taliesin is the name of the town Frank Lloyd Wright grew up in, but the etymology of Taliesin dates back to the 16th Century. It's the name of a famous Welsh manuscript." I never would have known that answer had I not walked in Wells' shoes. During the filming he kept asking me if I had read this book and that book, all obscure. "No, I haven't. No I haven't." He had to prove his superiority and that wasn't too hard for him to do. Notwithstanding, I was in the presence of a genius. The reason I tell you that story is because an inordinate number of executives are driven to show their superior knowledge. This is a pretty common trait with young entrepreneurs. It's such a turn off! During the filming he ordered this humungous bowl of ice cream. When it arrived, he said in a jocular manner, "My doctor told me to stop having intimate dinner parties for four unless there are three other people". That may be funny, but by now I was fed up.

Moral:

It doesn't take long before customers, employees and investors become fed up with a superiority attitude. Check yourself out before you're out. Down deep, everyone knows if they tend to want to be the leader of the band and show their talents off. They have a "know-it-all" persona because they believe they are smarter, even before they read the music sheet.

Orson was grossly overweight and not in the best of health. He died three days later. It has been said I was the last to film him. Hopefully, that doesn't say my directing skills are deathly.

John Wayne epitomized rugged masculinity both on and off the screen. He could never have become the icon that he became if his career had been associated with customer service relations. He was a perfectionist, but with horse-sense! There is a big difference between a perfectionist and one who is persistent. Persistency is a necessary virtue to business success. The first time we met, he greeted me with, "Pilgrim, hopefully you know what you're doing so you don't waste my time!"

Moral:

The moral of this story is: perfectionists are deleterious to a company's success because they do not have a time-clock in their heads and, therefore, they will stay too long on a project and opportunities will escape them. However, a persistent executive with horse sense is a golden asset!

Rodney Dangerfield was a fun guy, but he was never in the moment. If you want to influence someone, you need to be in the moment with them. Executives can't influence people if they are always saying things like: "Can't talk now.," "I'm rushing off to someplace." They allow themselves to be interrupted with calls. They limit their time with you by saying: "Talk fast, I'm in a hurry." Rodney was always doing his shtick, whereas Arthur Ashe made you feel that he wanted to be with you and hear what you wanted to say.

Moral:

Patience pays off in unexpected ways. Build your patience by reading, taking time to meditate, take a nap. President Kennedy would take a twenty-minute nap every working day. To the young executive on their way up I say, unequivocally, you must take time to read if you wish to be a better band-leader of your business orchestra.

Francis Albert Sinatra was the epitome of perseverance. The definition of perseverance is "persistency under fire . . . to persist in spite of difficulties." If you were to rank Perfection, Persistency and Perseverance, (all are different mental attitudes), I would rank Perseverance *Number One*. Sinatra was always having to reinvent himself. When his teen market was no longer there, he reinvented himself as a movie star. His early movies were box-office failures. He went on television with his own show, but his ratings were dwarfed by the Milton Berle Show. He was at his lowest ebb. He persevered by "calling in his favors" to play the role of Pvt. Angelo Maggio in the movie *From Here To Eternity*, for which he won an Academy Award. Once again, Sinatra resurrected his music career and became the Chairman of the Board.

William Shatner is the chameleon of perseverance. He continually reinvented himself from Star Trek to Boston Legal and a host of other shows in-between. Bill would greet you with an attitude of "I'm here to help you. I can act, sing, write, direct and pitch your product." Because he oozed confidence, it was easy for him to continually reinvent himself.

Moral:

Not only can you reinvent yourself, you can do the same for your business. Executives must multi-task; one eye focused on their core business and the other eye scans for changes in the marketplace. I'm not talking about adding another SKU; I'm talking about *Blue Oceans*, radical changes. We have all heard the axiom, "If you want to make a lot of money find a need and fill it." I would add to that:

find a problem and solve it. Look Up for *Pop-Ups* and small *Blue Oceans*.

When you are driving to work, I bet you see big, vacant retail stores and you say to yourself, "Who is ever going to rent that space? Certainly no one in this economy." That vacant space is a problem that needs a solution. Several real estate executives didn't see a problem, rather an opportunity. The *pop-up* retail concept is a great example of business reinvention.

A pop-up retail space is a venue that is empty. Manufacturers and retail merchandisers rent the vacant stores for short periods of time. Depending on the vendor, the space has multiple uses. The trend is called "*Pop-Up Retailing*" as these initiatives have a tendency to pop-up unannounced, quickly draw in the crowds, and then disappear or morph into something else. One month it may be Halloween costumes, a month later Christmas items. Ideal for selling Fall and Spring fashions. These stores, while small and temporary, can build up buzz by consumer exposure. *Pop-Ups* can bring inner-city chic to rural areas: from individual designers teaming up to real estate agents making better use of vacant properties, to big brands looking to add a bit of 'cool' and agility to their otherwise fixed locations and massive flagship stores.

Target, the US-based discount-chic franchise that works with (amongst others) fashion designer Isaac Mizrahi, opened up a temporary 1500 sq. feet store in Rockefeller Center to celebrate Mizrahi's stylish yet affordable, new women's clothing line. The glossy store was so successful that *Target* actually housed a temporary floating store on the Hudson River for the Christmas season. That's *Pop-Up Retailing* at its best!

Because these stores are able to rent their retail space at a fraction of the cost (filling unused retail space) they can offer their items at prices that are easy on the budget. The very nature of these "indie" boutiques means you will find fashions for the season and unique gifts priced to sell.

Another example of a *Pop-Up* that solves a problem is the concept of renting executive office space by the day. With the down-turn in the economy causing the commercial leasing of office space to come to a sudden stop, companies have popped-up with day rentals of executive offices. Most of these companies offer a 5-days-a-month plan for a low of $299 on a six-month lease. Keep looking for problems that your solution can solve. Be determined!

Giddyup

I find horse racing to be a snapshot of "*determination.*" The more determined the horse is, the more the Winner's Circle can be called "home." Racetrack pundits told the owner about the great thoroughbred Seabiscut, that the horse would never win anything. The horse was undersized, it had crooked legs and was knobby-kneed. Added to his physical infirmities, Seabiscuit was lazy and slept a lot. He had an inauspicious start, losing his first 14 races finishing way back in the pack. But the owner and trainer didn't give up; instead they relegated him to a punishing racing schedule to infuse determination. It worked! Seabiscuit became one of the most determined horses of all time. He went on to win the Triple Crown. Physicalities didn't keep him from winning nor should they keep you from winning.

The other great thoroughbred who epitomized perseverance was Secretariat. He was given the nickname "Big Red" because of his massive size and stature. They could have easily nicknamed him "Mr. Determination." His owner, Penny Tweedy, was equally determined. When you combine two positives, you get a winner every time. Penny, a housewife who inherited her father's farm, despite her lack of horseracing knowledge and against all odds, managed to navigate the male-dominated horseracing business with the help of veteran trainer, Lucien Laurin, ultimately fostering the first Triple Crown Winner in twenty-five years. There is a wonderful corollary here in this story. Take heed, you don't have to have all the answers and everything perfect to take action, but you must have determination. Go for it, because conditions will never be perfect.

She didn't take the first money that was offered even though she needed it. Nor should you. Determination doesn't have a price. If she had listened to all those dream busters and the horseracing elite, she would not have come to own a Triple Crown Winner." Secretariat was such a determined horse that he won the Belmont Stakes by 31 lengths. 40 years later, the time he ran the race in still stands. ESPN listed Secretariat as "One of the 100 Greatest Athletes of the 20th Century." When Secretariat died, necropsy revealed that his heart was twice the size of an ordinary horse. A "determined" heart is what we should strive for in any endeavor where we hope to win the race.

Conclusion:

First Impressions, in many cases, are previews of coming attractions. After the first meeting your ears and eyes may fool you, but your gut is not so easily deceived. My advice is to go with your gut feeling!

Good common sense: if time is of the essence, don't deal with a perfectionist. If a persistent person doesn't have "*horse-sense*," unbridle him and go your own way. If a procrastinator has yet to procrastinate, don't wait. "The man of decision can not be stopped. The one of indecision can not be started. Take your choice." Napoleon Hill

Sandpaper people, those who rub you the wrong way, will not change. Don't waste your valuable time. To you women who are reading this book, don't try to save a Sandpaper person; it will be like pushing a string. If Orson Welles lived and I continued to work with him, he would never have changed.

There are enough irritants in doing business, so why add sandpaper associates. My silver hair advice is to always strive to choose happiness in your business relationships. Being happy doesn't mean that everything will be perfect. Happiness is not the absence of problems but the ability to deal with them. Success is not the key to happiness; happiness is the key to success.

10th Commandment:
Thou Shall Raise Money by Awareness

The biggest challenge an entrepreneur and a business owner is faced with is raising money! It amazes me how many executives we meet who have not carefully prepared answers to the nine basic questions that investors will ask. In these times it's critical that you need to have thought out and rehearsed your answers in advance for these nine questions. Before I share with you what *not* to say, let me share with you what investors want to hear. You begin with your 120-second, high-powered, benefit-oriented "elevator pitch." Be dynamic! They are also buying off on you. Now that you have told them very succinctly what your product/service is, the VC or the Accredited Investor want answers to these (9) questions:

1. Why would someone want to buy your product?
2. Can you be "First" in your marketplace?
3. How are you going to sell the product?
4. How much money have you personally invested?
5. What intellectual properties do you have?
6. Does the company have the potential in three years or sooner to have revenue in the $20 to $60 million range?
7. Do you have a defined exit strategy that could be executed in three to five years?
8. What's my risk for making this investment? What's my reward?
9. Are the credentials of your management team bankable?

Today, more than ever, the VC is looking for a fundable team. That means you need more than a one-person team if you want money. If you can't convince people to join your company before you get venture capital, you won't be able to convince a VC to give you money.

The management team should possess relevant domain expertise and operating experience.

The VC/Investor wants to be assured that you have thought out your marketing plan with profitability in mind and a management team in place. There are three different types of capital you can get: early stage capital, expansion capital, and buyout capital. Before you start your dog and pony show, make sure you know what type of capital you are going after. If you are trying to raise a few hundred thousand dollars or a million dollars, you are better off pitching angel investors. Most VCs tend to shy away from investing small amounts of capital.

Over a fifty-year span I have produced the tools and drafted the strategies that have raised sizable sums of investment capital for clients. I've seen it all, from terrible presentations to spectacular ones. These years of experience have built a knowledge base which allows us to identify and chart what successful companies do and what unsuccessful companies fail to do.

For example: too many entrepreneurs, particularly in the tech world, get caught up in the engineering aspect of their product or service and fail to clearly define the size of their market and how they are going to reach their target market. I smile when an inventor or an engineer walks into my office because I know that he wants to tell me in great painstaking detail how his widget works. The end-user doesn't give a rat's ass if the cat is black or white or eats on schedule; he/she is only interested if it catches rats.

Make sure you don't say something stupid like you are going to get on TechCrunch and thousands of people will then come to your website. TechCrunch is a great site, but that isn't a marketing plan. Too often, a Venture Capitalist will find that almost all of the entrepreneur's brainpower has been concentrated on producing his or her new widget while the marketing side goes wanting. Weak target-marketing is a surefire way to get rejected by Venture Capitalists and Angel Investors.

"Are you smarter than a 5th Grader?" This is not a TV game show challenge; it's the level of understanding that you will want to present. If you can get a 5th grader to understand what you are doing, then an Angel Investor or a VC will understand what you are doing.

The Building Blocks for Raising Money Are The Four OPMs

Investors are scared to give money to people they don't know. If you don't know any investors, you better start getting to know them! You can easily do this by reading and commenting on their blog or by striking up an email conversation with them. Or, you could ask your friend or a lawyer if they can introduce you to a VC. Good lawyers know a ton of VCs. Notwithstanding, the cornerstones for raising capital are: OPM, OPE, OPM and OPI.

Everyone knows that the first acronym OPM stands for *Other People's Money*. If people are willing to invest, it confirms you have what others perceive to be a viable financial venture.

On the other hand, if no one is willing to invest it's a tell-tale sign that the entrepreneur should not invest any more money or time. Way too often the entrepreneur has fallen so deeply in love with their venture that he won't let go. They are convinced that everyone else is wrong. Be Cautious. Tenacity can be very expensive!

A great example of falling in love with a project that no one wanted to fund is John Wayne's persistence to fund the movie *The Alamo*. For fourteen years he looked for financial support to produce the movie. No studio would fund it. Wayne was so convinced that this movie would be a big, box-office blockbuster that he staked the production with his own money. Wrong! Wrong! It was the only movie John Wayne starred in that lost money. The pearl of wisdom that can be learned from this story is: If others won't play, get out of the sandbox."

The second, OPE, stands for *Other People's Experiences*. Seek out and contact the people who are experienced in the industry or venture you're going to enter into. Experience is great financial currency. People who are recognized as highly-experienced executives have a tendency to share their knowledge. I have found them to be willing mentors.

The third OPM stands for *Other People's Might*. The object here is to strategize how you can be seen in the company of highly-creditable executives, investors, lawyers, doctors, philanthropists. Why is that important? Because power-brokers will mentally conclude *Birds of a Feather Flock Together*.

Be courageous! Step-out of your station-in-life comfort zone and approach the business fraternity you want to rush. Show them what you can do! There was a man named Shakespeare, a pretty good writer wouldn't you say? Well, he had no credibility. During the Bard's lifetime, he was a play writer and therefore was not considered a serious author. Plays were for entertainment, poems were for the elite. Not only did he write plays, he was from Yeoman stock. (Basically from across the tracks, the wrong side of town). To gain credibility, he did what I am recommending you do: he sought out Marlowe and Sir Walter Raleigh, the great poets of the time and made friends with them. He even wrote a few poems so he would be more credible with the elite. The Shakespearian quote I love best and is very appropriate here is "Assume a virtue if you have it or not." Let nothing hold you back! Go for it!

The fourth acronym is OPI. It stands for *Other People's Influence.* Today, targeting influencers is seen as a means of amplifying the marketing message. Influencers come in many shapes and sizes: bloggers with larger social network contacts, political peddlers, industry analysts, bankers. Influencers are early-adopters. The want to tell people what is hot or not. There are now called *Trendformers.* Their role is to influence their circle of friends and associates. You need to connect with these *Trendformers* and have them use their influence to promote your fund-raising activities. I have an axiom that when I speak it, my wife cringes. "Never take a poor person to lunch." That results in her saying "Oh, where is your compassion?" Compassion has nothing to do with it. Only rich people with wealth and influence can make money for you, so take them to lunch! You get what I'm saying. The 19th commandment, Word of Mouse, goes into more depth about the dynamics of Influencers.

Here are the ten fund-raising commandments you should never violate:

1. ***Don't Dip the Vegetables in Chocolate.*** Don't sugarcoat your potential. Don't speculate to make the deal sweeter. All too often, VCs hear entrepreneurs claim that their innovative product will easily capture a 1% share of the market. The problem is that too many entrepreneurs foolishly assume that such a small milestone is easy to achieve. In truth, VCs know from experience that the vast majority of companies never gain 1% or more of their total marketplace. Don't make a sweeping market share, long-range claim; just tell the investor what you can do right now, a year from now and in five years.

2. ***Ye Who Cries Conservative Errs.*** Don't try to impress the VC by claiming that your estimates and projections are conservative. It's safe to assume that the venture capitalist has heard this hollow reassurance dozens of times and stopped listening some time ago. Make sure that what you are projecting is realistic and based on some kind of defendable data.

3. ***Don't Throw a Stone Mistake.*** Investors don't like it when you diss the competition. One of the most ill-advised statements an entrepreneur can make is: "Our product is so unique that we face little or no competition." The investor will shake his head, knowing there's always competition and the only question is whether or not you have some kind of competitive advantage that gives you a good shot at winning the sales wars. In short, failing to show respect for your competition is a serious mistake when wooing a VC or an accredited-investor.

4. ***The Who is Coming To Dinner Mistake.*** So you're planning to bring Michael Jordan, Steve Jobs, Alan Greenspan and former President, Bill Clinton onboard in the next six months. Don't bother telling that to angel investors or venture capitalists. That's a big mistake. In the mind of the VC, your current team is your team for the purposes of lining up financial backing. You need more than a one-person team if you want money. If you can't convince people to join your company before you get venture capital, you won't be able to convince a VC to give you money.

5. ***Tell the Whole Truth and Nothing But the Truth.*** To a VC, even little white lies are reason enough not to give you the money you need. Misleading a VC is not only an error, but it is one that is likely to be exposed very quickly. A venture capitalist is like a professional poker player in that he/she develops a highly-tuned ability to detect when someone is bluffing. Always disclose your current status. Prospective investors never like to find out during the due-diligence process that a company has two-times more accounts payable than cash.

6. ***The Invincible Patent Mistake.*** Remember, a patent is only as good as your ability to legally defend it and investors know that to be true. Even the best-patented process or product is no guarantee of success for an enterprise that hinges on dozens of

individual factors. The "sure thing" claim is a mistake. Claims of invincibility or inevitable success as the result of an existing or pending patent are unlikely to carry any weight with a VC.

7. ***You Talk Too Much Mistake.*** If you want to cause an investor to go deaf, just keep talking. Too many entrepreneurs talk until they are blue in the face and virtually spend no time listening to the investor's questions. If you have rehearsed beforehand, your answers will be concise and to the point.

Many years ago John Hooker wrote a popular song called *You Talk Too Much.* The lyrics go something like this:
You Talk Too Much, Baby
You Talk Too Much
You yak, yak, yak
You yak too much

I had a client who never stopped talking. He was a legend in talking customers out of buying his products. He couldn't understand why he wasn't closing sales. He would grumble, "I said everything I could think of." He would always say, "Funny, he didn't say much." I would then comment, "You didn't give him a chance to tell you what he wanted." My coaching was falling on deaf ears, so I resigned the account. On my way out, I gave his secretary a ringtone to install on his cell phone The ringtone played "You Talk Too Much."

8. ***The Telling Rather Than Showing Mistake.*** Remember, the most effective way to present your product is to *Show and Sell* and not just Tell. If you choose to show the proposed ads, I strongly recommend you Show and then Tell what problems these ads solve. Creativity in advertising is problem-solving. As philosopher, John Dewey, put it: "A problem well-stated is a problem half-solved."

9. ***You didn't Create An "Elevator Pitch That Takes You To The Top Floor.*** Compose a ninety-second, succinct explanation of your product/service: What the product does, what need does it fulfill, market size, and how much money you will need. Once written, rehearse your pitch time and time again so it becomes

second nature and you can command respect with tonality and confidence. If you don't rehearse, there will be no curtain call! Beware that a frequently-fatal error arises, most often when the VC asks a question and the responding entrepreneur concentrates on trying to head off what he or she thinks is the next question rather than simply answering the one at hand. This is another reason why you must rehearse beforehand.

10. *Not Anticipating All The Tough Questions VCs Will Probably Ask You.* In the 1st Commandment I shared the *Law of Predictability* with you and here is where it applies: you must anticipate every question that will be asked of you. Adopt the Mock-Jury scenario, have your friends and associates ask you challenging questions. Once you have determined what the predictable questions will be, prepare your answers to be persuasive. Give them back the answers they are looking for in order to give you the funds you are requesting. It's also of paramount importance that you have copies of your Business Plan available for distribution at the VC meeting. I personally believe that besides having your financials in the business plan, it's smart to have hand-out copies of the financials.

VIP: Make sure your business plan and collateral have been proofed. You will immediately lose credibility if words are not spelled correctly or the grammar is poor. You should come to the table with all relevant details about your management team, definition of the product or service, the market, the perceived need, how you will meet it and justification and use of funds. I wish you well!

N.B. If you are going after "accredited investors," I have found that those investors will sooner watch a ten-minute video than read and evaluate a 2-inch-thick, printed Business Plan. Over the years, I have been very successful in converting a company's Business Plan into a ten-minute video (Not the PPM). That convergence has resulted in raising a great deal of money for our clients. Although the paradigms of several business models have changed in the last ten years as a result of the dramatic influence of the Internet, the Net has demonstrated its power to accelerate failure as well as success. What has *not* changed are the nine (9) basic questions VCs and accredited investors will ask and attack you with. Now that cash is tight, these challenges are more relevant than ever.

The Battle Plan

Being an advocate and admirer of Sun Tzu's principles, the fund-raising battle plan is framed in military analogies. The boardroom is the battlefield.

Oops! No More Money For Bullets

Imagine if we were in a war and the U.S. Government announced that "We have to stop the war now. We just ran out of money to make bullets and missiles." One of the most deadly sins is to have insufficient capital to grow the company. Even VCs will ask: "Is there enough money to grow the business beyond the dream state?" Here's where your Board of Advisors will be a great help in determining the capital requirements to meet the company's monthly benchmarks. More companies fail because of insufficient cash than for any other reason. This is not only true for start-ups, but also for companies that are going to be manufacturing or launching a new product line.

The company, in the early-growth stage, is very vulnerable to the other side of the same coin: namely, excessive debt and overhead. Debt service can destroy a start-up and paralyze an established company. That's the reason you must stick to your Business Plan and don't let greed and glory exceed budget or planned expenditures. The bottom line: make sure you have enough capital to wage a successful sales battle and win the war.

You Don't Have A Battle Plan

You wouldn't go to war without bullets because there would be no way to protect yourself. It would be equally suicidal if you went into business without a Business Plan. The best thing about a good business plan, from an entrepreneur's point of view, is that it helps in organizing his/her thought processes. You must have a critical path chart of targets.

Zig Zigler tells a simple story that dramatizes the importance of having a target. Howard Hill was probably the greatest archer who ever drew a bowstring. After sending the first arrow to the center of the bull's eye, he would then literally split that arrow with his next shot. He could hit the bull's eye five-hundred times in a row because he had a target to aim at. As great as Howard Hill was, if you were to blindfold him and then spin him around so he would have no idea which direction he was facing, how on earth could he hit a target that he couldn't see? The answer is: he couldn't. Once you took away his target he was a mere mortal. A question you should ask yourself is: "How can I hit a target that I can't see?" Do you expect to be more accurate than Howard, who has a defined target and you don't? Every business warrior must have a defined target in mind to be successful. Here's the best question: "What are you doing to guarantee your failure?" I said *failure*. It's amazing the insight that question will reveal to you.

The very nature of an entrepreneur is to constantly evaluate new ideas and business strategies. Without targets to control these outbursts of creativity, chaos can consume a business. With a good Business Plan, you can look at your ideas and say, "Hey, this just doesn't fit right now."

The Enemy Will Not Attack

Oh yes, enemies *will* attack. If the company is making money, their marketing guns will roar. You must be prepared in advance. You dig the well before you're thirsty. In the excitement of launching a product or a new service, management can overlook establishing a line of defense, a fall-back position against the perils of doing business. In a competitive environment, it's abundantly clear that you must have four primary defense strategies:

First Defense, dig in and establish a limited-liability entity, such as a Corporation or an LLC. Register and copyright everything that moves. Have a stack of NDAs handy.

Second Defense, get everything in writing. No handshakes or oral agreements. A written contract is a bullet-proof shield that not only protects you, but your suppliers and vendors. Make sure to write in the provision that if a dispute arises, the prevailing party will be reimbursed for legal fees in every contract you draft.

Third Defense, obtain adequate business insurance. Do not, and I emphasize, *do not*, start-up your company without insurance. I'll bet if you were to ask one hundred small business owners whose annual sales volume is $2,000,000 if they had the proper insurance protection, the majority will probably say, "Unfortunately, I don't!" Make sure you do. When you raise the money, you must include adequate funds to buy product liability insurance, officer identification, errors & omissions policies.

Fourth Defense, imagine you're a small company with a "hot," successful product. You're first to market. Now, imagine that another company, a much bigger company with much greater financial resources, comes out with a similar product to yours that infringes on your patent. Your attorney tells you "don't worry, you have a strong patent, registered trademark and copyright." That may be true, but the harsh reality is nine out of ten times you probably won't be able to afford to litigate against the better-financed opponent. Get insurance that pays for your legal fees. These policies are called "intellectual property abatement/enforcement." Your adversary will usually back away.

Those are the 4 basic defenses. Lets now discuss what's your offense should have!

A Sounding Board of Generals

Sun Tzu always had three ABC generals reporting to him: **A**rchery, **B**attalions and **C**avalry. Most importantly, he granted them the power to advise him. You'll be talking to yourself if you don't have a Board of Advisors. Every company needs a minimum of three advisors to get through the land mines of the first six months and the next two years.

What I recommend is an ABC Board of Advisors:

"A" stands for Attorney	The Attorney must be experienced in Business Law. He will be an invaluable asset.
"B" stands for Businessman	A Management and/or Sales Consultant. What I definitely recommend is for you to contact the local SCORE office (Counselors to America's Small

Business). This is a powerful resource. SCORE has more than 12,000 business counselors representing more than 600 business skills. These volunteers are retired corporate leaders and business owners who will share their wisdom with you at no cost. It's Free!

"C" stands for CPA   Notwithstanding that the Company will have a finance person, the Board needs a CPA to give valuable second opinions. One of the best ways to use his finance acumen is to have him pre-qualify your business' spending decisions.

Before every major purchase, investment, or hiring, take the time to ask your Advisory Board to help you answer the following questions:

1. Is this expenditure necessary right now?
2. Will this make money or cost the company money?
3. Is there a less-expensive way to accomplish this goal?
4. Do you think we should outsource? Lease? Hire?

Fat Centurions Never Won a Battle

Stay lean and mean. Fat centurions never won a battle. If your initial infrastructure resembles the *Pillsbury Doughboy*, you're weighted to fail. Too often many entrepreneurs have the tendency to bring the "*infrastructure bloat*" from their previous corporate careers to their start-up and they fail because they added too many employees too soon. Curb that appetite, stick to the Business Plan and if the addition of employees and added expenditures are not budgeted for, forget about it. Stay lean and mean and you will survive.

Tell Them How The Battle Ends

You must have a defined Exit Strategy. Today, "How do I get out?" is the number one question investors will ask. Investors will put money in if you tell them how they will get it back into their pocketbooks. It's an era of capital preservation! The majority of first-round investors want to see that you have a 3-to-5-year Exit Strategy. Your Exit Strategy will influence many decisions you make. Are you going public? Are you grooming the company to be acquired by a competitor? Are you looking for a reverse merger, a reporting shell or are you establishing a family legacy?

Don't Make Milli Vanilli a General

You cannot give lip service to your product and expect to stay in business. A good example of this is Milli Vanilli, the 80's Duo who were a sensation until they revealed that they were only lip-synching their songs. Then it was over, never to be resurrected. That is exactly what happens when you have sizzle and there's no steak. Once your customers feel that you haven't been honest with them, they flee from you. We've seen companies fail because the initial hype exceeded the customer's demand for the product. Successful companies deliver more than what was promised to the consumer. To create a business with staying power, you need a product of substance or a service that provides value. Budget as much for market research as you do for advertising and promotions.

Conclusion

By avoiding the 7 Deadly Sins, you will be way ahead of the game. You'll be on the right road to success and if you do encounter speed bumps and potholes in the road, you'll be able to avoid their consequences. Remember that the four OPMs are the cornerstone for you to get funding. Unexpected things usually happen, so make sure the dollar amount you're asking for is large enough to account for them. Make sure you have the proper insurance.

After your presentation is over, you are going to get bombarded with questions. There is no way you can be prepared for all of the questions. Just be honest and have faith in yourself. If you know your business like the back of your hand, you shouldn't have any problems. There are 9 questions that the investors will surely ask you, They never change. That's good news because you can prepare and practice. Once again, it's worth repeating. Here are the nine FAQs to be prepared for:

1. Why would someone want to buy your product?
2. Can you be "First" in your marketplace?
3. How you are going to sell the product?

4. How much money have you personally invested?
5. What intellectual properties do you have?
6. Does the company have the potential in 3 years or sooner to have revenue in the $20 to $60 million range.
7. Do you have a defined exit strategy that could be executed in 3-to-5 years?
8. What's my risk for making this investment? What's my reward?
9. Are the credentials of your management team bankable?

If you believe deep-down that you are prepared to answer the nine (9) big ones and you trust in prayer, the money will come! There is more money on the street for a good deal than you can imagine.

11th Commandment: Thou Shall Come To Know He Who Laughs . . . . Lasts!

Why would I think one of the great commandments in business and life is *Thou Shall Come To Know He Who Laughs . . . Lasts?* The reason is that I have seen executives burn out, stress to the detriment of the company and lose their families because they couldn't laugh. They couldn't see fun in anything they were doing. I guarantee that two unpleasant things are going to happen: your health will deteriorate and so, too, will your business.

Laughter is the fountain of both personal and business longevity, yet too few executives drink from the fountain. Are you myopic with work and don't have time for humor? Look in the mirror and question yourself. Are you lighthearted or frowning? Are you cheerfully optimistic or pessimistic? Do people really enjoy being in your company. Many executives aren't aware that humor is rooted in confidence. Humor may allow a person to feel in control of a situation and make it seem more manageable. It allows people to release fear, anger and stress, all of which can harm the body over time. Humor improves the quality of life.

If business is going bad and you're stressed out, there's a natural tendency to become depressed. Depression is the most prominent mental health issue in society today. There are a host of "treatment" suggestions that flood the media and internet. One such treatment is humor, which focuses on increasing laughter and smiling. Smiling is a painless and free treatment, but can these simple motor movements be enough to have an effect on mental health? Recent studies suggest that smiling *does* have a measurable influence on emotions. Laughter appears to change brain chemistry and may boost the immune system. It definitely helps to stabilize blood pressure, thereby dramatically decreasing your tension! Robin Williams starred in the movie Patch Adams, a fact-based story of Dr. Adams who successfully helped patients recover their health by interjecting humor into their patient's care. His prescription was "A laugh a day keeps the stress away."

Humor has always played a major role in my life. In Commandment #1, I told you that my MBA thesis was written about the "Alacrity of a Joke," which begot the *Law of Predictability*. In my ministry of encouragement, I have come to know humor is a prayer waiting to be shared. In my early career I had an opportunity to write a few two-liners for Rodney Dangerfield and Tom Poston, a sidekick of Bob Newhart. For Rodney I wrote the following zingers:

* I'm so henpecked I cackle in my sleep.
* I bought my wife a mink, She keeps the cage real clean.

Now you know why I didn't become a professional comedy writer. To keep you rolling in the aisle with side-splitting laughter, let me share a zinger I wrote for Tom Poston:

* There's one thing good about Alzheimer's: you can hide your own Easter Eggs. (Boo)

Let's get back to my *Stress Less* prescription. The main ingredient would be encouragement. The direction on the label says you must encourage three people every day for one month. Side effect: your heart will swell with happiness and you'll be smiling more. For any medication to work, you must exercise. Here's what I would recommend:

* Exercise your smile muscles each morning while you brush your teeth. Make happy faces. All athletes know that warming muscles up is the key to getting maximum use from them.
* Develop an internal "smile file" of images and thoughts. My smile file includes taking people who think they are too professional or too conservative to act like a clown to a children's ward in a hospital. No training needed! Once they don the

clown clothes and put on the rubber noses, their personalities change forever—for the better.

* In your mental exercise gym, it's mandatory that you work out an encouragement antenna, an antenna that is always up, listening for an opportunity to encourage someone.

Smiling and laughing are antidotes that you need to inoculate yourself with because they will make you feel better about yourself, and help you to become a more enjoyable person for your business associates, customers, friends and family to be around. It's all because you have unlocked the incredible power of staying in a good mood almost every single minute of the day, regardless of what's going on in your life.

When I talk to executives about humor being the sunshine of their business mind, it's usually followed with the question "How do I change?" My answer is: evaluate the positive and negative words you habitually use. Words make us laugh and cry. They can wound or heal; they can give us hope or despair. The power of words can transform our noblest intentions! Check yourself out. Words are the vessels of change. Look carefully at the words you habitually choose to use when it comes to worker relations, talking to your spouse and the words you use to evaluate your own self. You'll find that you will probably approach all three relationships in different ways. If you discover that the words you use are *not* positive and encouraging to all three, then you should change your habitual vocabulary. Aristotle said, "The whole is greater than the sum of its parts." Your business and personal relationships will all experience a new growth.

To accomplish this new growth, you will need to do two things: First, invest the time to self-evaluate your habitual positive and negative vocabulary. Be hard on yourself. Habits are hard to break. At first, habits are like cobwebs, then cables. Habit, if not resisted, soon becomes a necessity. Any time you sincerely want to change, raise your standard. Demand more of yourself.

We live in a butt-tight business world and everything has to be proven first before action can take place. One Sunday at church I saw a small girl at her play table, drawing with crayons. I asked her, "What are you drawing?" The little girl said, "God." I said, "How can you draw God? Nobody has ever seen him. Nobody knows what he looks like." The little girl looked up at me and said, "They'll know when I finish this!" Just like that little girl, when you finish your prescription of laughter, people will see what a transformed person looks like.

If you can't see how adopting what might seem to you as a frivolous, Pollyanna approach will help to resolve your sleepless nights and stressful days, I feel sorry for you. People want to do business with people they like. Family relationships dissolve when there's no happiness.

Management Benefits of Laughter:

- **Perspective**: Studies show that our response to stressful events can be altered by whether we view something as a 'threat' or a 'challenge'. Humor can give us a more lighthearted perspective and help us to view events as 'challenges', thereby making them less threatening and more positive.

- **Social Benefits**: Laughter connects us with others. It is also contagious, so if you bring more laughter into *your* life, you can most likely help others around you to laugh more and realize these benefits as well. By elevating the mood of those around you, you can reduce their stress levels, and perhaps improve the quality of social interaction you experience with them, reducing your stress level even more!

- **Management Style**: Pay intention to this insight. If you're a marketing executive aged fifty plus you need to understand that the Y generation won't work for you if your management style creates stress. This is the *"privileged"* generation and they don't want to work in a business environment filled with stress. They have seen their dads come from work out of sorts, with little or no humor. They don't want that scenario in their lives.

* **Distraction**: Laughter brings the focus away from anger, guilt, stress and negative emotions in a more beneficial way than other mere distractions.

* **Hormones**: Laughter reduces the level of stress hormones like *cortisol,* and *epinephrine.* It also increases the level of health-enhancing hormones like endorphins and neurotransmitters. Laughter increases the number of antibody-producing cells and enhances the effectiveness of T cells. What does that mean? It means your

immune system will become stronger, and you'll have fewer physical effects stemming from stress.

How To Use Laughter:

Laughter is one of my all-time favorite stress-management strategies. You can get more laughter in your life with the following:

- It pays to use humor as a negotiating strategy to mitigate conflict. Humor has a way of uniting even the most diverse participants.
- Instead of complaining about life's frustrations, try to laugh about them. Warren Buffet is quite humorous when you have a private moment with him. He believes life should be approached in a mirthful way. If you have wealth without health, you're a poor person.
- You're not going to change overnight, so "Fake It Until You Make It." Here's some encouraging news: research studies show that the positive effects of smiling occur whether the smile is fake or real. Faked laughter also provides the benefits mentioned above. So, smile more and if you need to fake laughter, you'll still achieve positive effects and the fake merriment may lead to real smiles and laughter.
- On the home front get involved with you kids' activities. Cheer them on! When you're their cheerleader, you become your own best friend. It's impossible to frown when you smile.

If Old McDonald Had An Advertising Farm

On that farm he would have a duck, a lizard, a bunny, two frogs, two chimpanzees, a purple cow, a tiger named Tony and a flatulent Clydesdale. I'm a big believer in the positive effects of humor in business and in advertising. It's my contention that humorous advertising resonates very well with consumers. They remember the sales message. I love the AFLAC Duck, the Geico Lizard, and the Energizer Bunny. The Duck has accomplished its goal by getting everyone to know the company's new name. The Lizard was equally successful. The Bunny was able to differentiate the Energizer battery from all others.

Every year when USA Today ranks the popularity of the Super Bowl commercials, the highest-ranked are the humorous commercials like Bud Light and Pepsi. Clearly, there are valid reasons for the use of humor in advertising. Granted, not every product or service lends itself to a humorous approach, but those that do become top of the mind.

What frustrates me is when an advertising agency produces a commercial just for shock value. For example: The flatulent Budweiser Clydesdale lifts its tail, ignites a gaseous emission and blasts the make-up off the blonde's face. How does that trigger a thirst for beer? Using pretty girls and double entendres isn't a crime, but it doesn't sell product. Carl's Jr., a regional fast-food chain, pushes the envelope to the limit. They have produced TV commercials that have had bad boy, Dennis Rodman, and Playboy owner, Hugh Hefner munching on Carl's Jr. six-dollar hamburgers with sexual overtures like: "Chickens don't have nuggets" and "This a real man's burger." Their agency produced a very sensual commercial of a beautiful young woman riding a mechanical bull in a very sexy gyrating motion as she eats the six-dollar burger. I'm all for edgy, but if the spot doesn't make you hungry and wanting to go the restaurant, other than for sex, it missed its mark.

Be very cautious! If you're of the mindset that you want to achieve "top of the mind" with shocking ads, you must take into account how many "would-be customers" will be offended and turned-off. A great example of viewers being turned off was when Desperate Housewives star, Nicolette Sheridan, committed a personal foul on Monday Night Football for Unnecessary Exposure. In the skit, NFL player Terrell Owens is about to leave the locker room to join his teammates when he is confronted by the terry-clothed Sheridan, who begs him to forego the football game for a locker-room romp. T.O. initially gives her a stiff arm, but the she drops the towel and a naked Sheridan winds up in his arms. T.O exclaims, "Aw hell, the team is going to have to go without me!" ABC was inundated with hundreds of enraged phone callers. What a terrible message: Do what feels good and not what your job is. Indianapolis Colts head coach, Tony Dungy, said, "I'm very disappointed in ABC for what took place on Monday Night Football. I have a twelve-year-old son who does his homework early on Monday to watch the game and he and many other young kids were exposed to this salacious garbage. That's infuriating." No one won, certainly not ABC, Monday Night Football, or the TV show Desperate Housewives.

An interesting study surveyed the creative directors of the top 150 Advertising Agencies and here is what they said:

1. Humor creates a positive mood that enhances persuasion.
2. Humor may aid persuasion to switch brands.
3. Humorous Commercials only work if they are really funny, otherwise death.
4. Humor in direct-mail and newspapers is not usually effective.
5. Humor does not aid source credibility.
6. Humor may distract from the brand and its attributes.
7. Humor is one of the best ways to achieve top-of-mind.

Audiences that are younger, better educated, upscale, male and professional are best-suited to humor. Older, less educated and downscale groups are least suited to humor. Consumer non-durables and business services are best-suited to humor. Corporate advertising and industrial products are least-suited. Humor should not be used with sensitive goods and services. The one thing that everyone agrees on is humor can be difficult to produce. It must be really funny or it will be death to the campaign. So test and test again. If the viewers laugh with you, it's a hit, usually a big hit. When they laugh at you, you're in big trouble.

Conclusion: When you applaud like you mean it, you cannot help but smile and chuckle. Just the act of clapping can awaken your body and senses. Clapping makes you feel happy and joyous! Remember that favorite kiddies' song: "If you're happy and you know it, clap your hands." **So give yourself a hand as you begin your day!**

12th Commandment:
Thou Shall Ditch PowerPoint

The aim of this commandment is to give you an awareness of the changing times when it comes to PowerPoint presentations. Millions of presentations are now given everyday with the aid of PowerPoint or other slideware, yet most presentations remain mind-numbingly dull, something to be endured by both presenter and audience alike. Presentations are generally ineffective, not because presenters lack intelligence or creativity, but because they have learned bad habits and lack awareness and knowledge about what makes for a great presentation and what does not. The typical slide presentation of today consists of a presenter reading streams of information that is already printed on the slides. That type of Power Point is old school. Ditch it. Why is it passé? Because of two major reasons: First, is redundancy. What you have is a presenter who keeps turning around to read the slides. Wrong! The purpose of PowerPoint's slides is to highlight and punctuate what the speaker is saying. Anyone can read, especially the audience. Second, compounding the redundancy is management's tendency to put too much copy on a slide. Way too much copy dooms the presentation. I would definitely recommend using pictures in the presentation to get the points across better. That way the audience becomes mentally involved, not just sitting there.

I'm always asked "what kind of pictures are we talking about?" For example, let's say a speaker is explaining to dentists about its company's 12-step procedure to collect late-paying accounts receivables quickly. The slides have the 12 steps spelled out in detail. One has to go. Replace the copy details with pictures of Dentists enjoying the benefits and let the speaker talk the sales points.

Professionally done, you can create a dull and dry presentation and make it dynamic. It's a three-step pitch format:

Step #1 is to "*Sell the Pain.*" You're trying to sell Dentists your receivable services. I would therefore have pictures depicting the financial pain of slow payments, and having to write them off, et al.

Step #2 is to "*Sell the Relief*" with applicable pictures (for example, Ethnic range of Dentists smiling and happy staff members beaming).

Step #3 is to "*Sell the Action.*" You must close with a call-to-action. Tell the audience what you want them to do to receive the relief from the pain. 95% of PowerPoint presentations fail to have a call-to-action on the screen. What usually happens is the speaker finishes his/her laundry list of benefits and asks the audience, "Any questions?" Wrong! The last thing the audience should hear and see is a precise call-to-action telling them what to do!

If we desire to communicate with more clarity, integrity and persuasiveness, then we must move beyond what is considered to be normal to something different and far more effective. Since people cannot read and listen well at the same time, then death to PowerPoint that includes lines of text projected on a screen that mirrors the spoken word of the presenter. It's about time that we recognize that putting the same information on a text form that is coming out of a speaker' mouth usually does not help but, in fact, hurts the message!

Make slides that reinforce your words, not repeat them. Create slides that demonstrate, with emotional proof, that what you're saying is true, not just accurate. No more than six words on a slide. There is no presentation so complex that this rule needs to be broken.

Here is a powerful example: Let's say it's very important to emphasize the point that we will be swimming with "*Sharks*" and we will need to be prepared. This slide serves to enhance the speaker's spoken words and triggers the mind to see the danger!

Amplification Through Simplification

Most people in business today would not have been exposed to the idea of making a visual stronger by stripping it down to its essence. There's a global presentation phenomenon that originated in Tokyo called Pech-Kucha. The Pecha-Kucha method of presentation of design and delivery is very simple. The object is to allow more time for the Q & A. Please understand as I explain this methodology that I'm not saying in any way that this is what you should be doing, but it's a sign of the times you should be aware of. It's a powerful snapshot of the future. Here's how it works: you must have 20 slides, each shown for 20 seconds, as you tell your story in sync with the visuals. That's 6 minutes and 40 seconds. Slides advance automatically and when done, you're done. That's it. Sit down. The objective of these simple but tight restraints, is to keep the presentation brief and give more time to answering probing questions. Even if you do not use the method, it's a great exercise for clarity and brevity.

Less always equals better communication. Although this is the conceptual age, too many times I have heard bosses say: "Where are all those bullet points? Where's the company logo?" Simplicity is powerful and leads to greater clarity, yet it is neither simple nor easy to achieve. Here are some pointers to make your presentation audience applause-worthy.

How to improve immediately

The bar is so low that improving in small, "open-minded" steps will make a big difference.

First, when you're preparing a presentation ask yourself two questions: "What's my point? Why does it matter to the audience?" Let the answers to those two question rule your writing. Here's where people stumble. Answering "Why does it matter?" seems so obvious to the presenter that they need to make it explicit. Yet, that is exactly what the audience is hoping and praying that you tell them.

Second, don't use cheesy images or clip art. Use professional, stock photo images. They are not expensive (ShutterStock.com). Don't use mundane images that are commonly used by the masses. For example, images like two hands shaking signifying agreement is trite and boring.

Third, for financial or technical presentations no dissolves, spins or other transitions. Keep it basic! On the other hand, if the audience consists of salespeople, entrepreneurs or small business owners, use interesting transitions, but not to the degree that they are "noise/ clutter" makers. Keep it simple!

Fourth, create a written document, a leave-behind. Put in as many footnotes or details as you like. Then, when you start your presentation tell the audience that you're going to give them all the details of your presentation after it's over and they don't have to write down everything you say. Remember, the presentation is to make an emotional sale. The document is the proof that helps the intellectuals in your audience accept the idea that you've sold them on emotionality.

Never ever hand out copies of your slides and certainly not before your presentation. That is the kiss of death. By definition, since slides are "speaker-support material," they are there in support of the speaker . . . YOU. As such, they should be completely incapable of standing by themselves and are thus useless to give to your audience where they will simply be guaranteed to be a distraction. The flip side of this is that if the slides can stand by themselves, why the heck are *you* up there in front of them?

Fifth, Keep the lights on; there is no good reason for turning them off. Today the projectors have the light amps shine bright enough to see the slides but, more importantly, the speaker. Talking about light, a presentation is never just about the facts. Less is more. Empty space is not nothing; it is a powerful something. Many times, empty space provides great clarity on the point

Sixth, who says your logo should be on every slide? Try removing logos from all except the first and last slide. The logo won't help make a sale or make a point, but what it does do is create clutter (noise). The logo is irrelevant and makes the presentation visuals look like a commercial.

Know Your SNR Ratio

SNR (Signal vs Noise) is the ratio of relevant to irrelevant elements of information in a slide. Noise is the irrelevant. The Signal is the relevant. The goal is to have the highest signal-to-noise ratio possible by eliminating the superfluous in your power-point slides and your flip chart. Aiming for a higher SNR is an attempt to make it easier for people to understand.

Caution: There is a diminishing effectiveness when you strip the slide too much. A major fish seller in NYC wanted to increase sales, so he hired a Madison Avenue Counseling Firm. Wrong right there. The consultant spent the day giving "keen-eye for the obvious" suggestions. At the end of the day, the consultant asked the owner to step outside and look at his sign that read: "*Fresh Fish Sold Here Daily*". There's too much clutter. He explained: "You can get rid of the word "Daily." A customer can see that you're open for business today." The sign now reads *Fresh Fish Sold Here*. The next clutter you need to remove is "Sold Here." Customers know your selling fish here. Of course you're selling fish. The sign now reads "*Fresh Fish.*" Here's where the logic starts a downward trend. Why say "Fresh?" What do people think you are selling? Fish that's not fresh? Now the sign reads just *"Fish"*. Look where you're selling. It's in the Financial District where the boats unload the fresh fish daily. So you don't need the word "Fish". Just put on a smile and let the aroma of the fish attract people. That will be $1,200, please.

Conclusion: Presenting with slides is so much a part of our culture now that people can hardly imagine preparing for a meeting and presenting at that meeting without slides. If the presenter is excellent, then I would save the PowerPoint for the Question & Answer period. If you use slideware in your next talk, aim to design and deliver a high SNR with the naturalness of a story teller, with simplicity. To accomplish this, follow my three (3) step PowerPoint Pitch format:

1. **Sell the Pain**
2. **Sell the Relief**
3. **Sell-the Call-to-Action.**

A word of advice: Never keep turning around *just* to read the copy on the slide. Only turn around if you're explaining a point you need to zero in on with a PowerPoint pen light.

V.I.P. Please understand that I'm not implying in any way that you shouldn't use slides with succinct bullet points My point is that you should filter picture slides throughout the PowerPoint presentation to give the salient points more impact and understanding to what you are saying.

The mediocre Presenter . . . tells.
The good Presenter . . . explains.
The great Presenter . . . inspires.

13th Commandment:
Thou Shall Give to Get

The Give-to-Get method is a formula. If you understand how it works, it will work for you every time. It's an identifying process, a syllogism, a theorem, whatever word you want to use to define the order of the steps a person needs to take to make a buying decision. It begins with you determining from the outset what you believe the consumer needs to know to accomplish his/her buying decision. Then you're going to supply, free, the knowledge they will need to know but not the How. *You* are the How!

This Commandment is all about new lead-generation. Let me share with you what I have found to be an excellent method for generating new customers for clients.

About two years ago I decided, literally overnight, to shift my emphasis totally. I decided to stop selling and start giving. If you can understand this paradox, then this is your lucky day. I am going to share the one piece of knowledge on marketing and business success that has produced exceptional sales in this roller-coaster economy. The principle can be summarized in the philosophy: "I don't want anything from you in return. I'm not selling you anything. I just want you to have this valuable information, free, to grow your business."

Not only do I recommend this "Give to Get" action philosophy to the clients for whom I consult, I have made it the fulcrum of my own lead-generating strategy. My commitment is to give, give and give again. In return, my lead-generation has increased significantly.

St. Francis of Assisi said it best "For it's in giving that we receive." I started by giving valuable information to prospects who could use it to help their business grow. As a matter-of-fact, that was my inspiration to write this book. Prior to this new *"giving marketing"* strategy, I would send prospects information about my business successes and say I can achieve the same for you. That's the traditional way and there's nothing wrong with that approach. Instead, I stopped using the "I can grow your business and solve your marketing problems, why don't you become my "client" pitch, with the "Giving to Get" approach. Within a couple of months, people to whom I had given ideas and marketing solutions started contacting me asking me to help them implement the concepts I had given them.

What had changed? I switched my focus from what I wanted to get to what they wanted. Instead of trying to convince people that my skill set would solve their *pain*, I provided them with some *relief* from the information I had sent them. Basically, I let them decide for themselves. Some became clients, some didn't. It really didn't matter because I knew I was making a difference and, in turn, my business was growing. Giving opens the way to receiving.

I learned some profound lessons. The first is that in business, as in life, *giving* is a great experience. The ones who give get back in kind. The second lesson was that most businesses wait until a client or customer gives them money before they start adding value to that customer's life. Now I say "Why wait?" Start adding value now and believe me, the customers will come to you.

So here's my very strong suggestion to you. Take this concept and try it out in your business for thirty days and see what happens. It's one of the most powerful marketing concepts on earth and yet it will cost you absolutely nothing. Decide for the next forty-five days that the prime purpose of your marketing efforts is to add incredible value to the lives of your present and future customers.

Forget about you and just focus on them. Step into their shoes and do whatever you can to enhance the quality of their business lives. Surprise them. Shock them. Make them laugh. Give them something they weren't expecting for free. Brighten up their day. Buy them a Cappuccino, anything that lets them know that their well-being is your top priority. The result is that you will differentiate yourself so massively from the mass of mediocrity out there, I think you may be surprised and, quite possibly, stunned at the results.

The phrase 'win-win' is very over-used these days but, if you are willing to give it a go, this strategy is true win-win. Your customers get an amazing and unprecedented experience from being in your presence, and your working day becomes a blast because everyone who interacts with you enjoys your company.

Over the years, I have been fortunate enough to spend time with some of the great marketers who could make the cash register ring. When I meet these individuals, I question them in great detail about what created their success. When you do this, something surprising soon becomes apparent: the prime driving force behind their success is not just the desire to make money. It is certainly one of the driving forces, but it is not *the* prime driving force.

At some level, it is a deep desire to make a real difference in the lives of the people they reach, to impact them in some way. To make a real difference. Don't get me wrong, Gates, Buffet and Branson, they love profits, but they're also smart enough to know that it was their passion for making a difference that brought in those profits in the first place. We're so immersed in working out how to increase sales and grow our businesses rather than in how to improve our own lives that we're missing the obvious way to do it, and it's right in front of us. The irony is that, if there is a secret to your success, it is to stop worrying about your success and start thinking about the success of your customers and potential customers. Pay attention to their problems, their needs. Go out of your way to make their lives easier, to put a bit of joy into their lives. Kahlil Gibran, the author of *The Prophet*, wrote, "You give little when you give of your possessions. It's when you give of yourself that you truly give."

When I'm talking to young people about the importance of giving and results, I tell this story to dramatize the point: What Goes Around, Comes Around!

His name was Fleming and he was a poor Scottish farmer. One day, while trying to make a living for his family, he heard a cry for help coming from a nearby bog. He dropped his tools and ran to the bog.

There, mired to his waist in black muck, was a terrified boy, screaming and struggling to free himself. Farmer Fleming saved the lad from what could have been a slow and terrifying death.

The next day, a fancy carriage pulled up to the Scotsman's sparse surroundings. An elegantly-dressed nobleman stepped out and introduced himself as the father of the boy Farmer Fleming had saved. "I want to repay you," said the nobleman. "You saved my son's life."

"No, I can't accept payment for what I did," the Scottish farmer replied waving off the offer. At that moment, the farmer's own son came to the door of the family hovel.

"Is that your son?" the nobleman asked. 'Yes,' the farmer replied proudly. "I'll make you a deal. Let me provide him with the level of education my own son will enjoy. If the lad is anything like his father, he'll no doubt grow to be a man we both will be proud of." And that he did. Farmer Fleming's son attended the very best schools and. in time, graduated from St.Mary's Hospital Medical School in London. He went on to become known throughout the world as the noted Sir Alexander Fleming, the discoverer of Penicillin.

Years afterward, the same nobleman's son who was saved from the bog was stricken with pneumonia. What saved his life this time? *Penicillin.* The name of the nobleman? Lord Randolph Churchill. His son's name? Sir Winston Churchill.

This is great story for a storyteller. (Commandment #5)

I now want to share a *"giving"* marketing strategy that I have been advising my small-business clients to use to attract potential customers and it works! You send out 750 emails at a time to people who could use their services or knows someone who could benefit from using their services. The information is free and topical.

To make this strategy work, the content must be useful and something you would pay for. Although the information is valuable, right off the top 50% won't open the emails. Of the 50% (375) who open and read the information, probably only 1% (at best, 2 people) may call to learn more. But here is the secret: you email those 750 people two more times with fresh, pertinent information. Then the magic starts to take place. By the fourth mailing, on average, more than 60 people will hit replay and possibly send you a very nice email thanking you for the flow of free valuable information you have been sending. This strategy should generate at least 8 or more new qualified customers. How cool is that!

The proof of the pudding is in the eating. Does this really work? At every conference or trade show I attend, people whom I have sent a flow of marketing tips and sales strategies will come up to me and say: "Hey, you're the guy who has been sending me all those marketing ideas. I want to thank you." But how can you make any money if you give it away free? I smile inwardly and you now know why. What could be better? I'm talking to that potential customer and he likes me. I'm confident we will do business!

The "Give to Get" philosophy has two-prongs on the "Get" side. Although it's pretty clear that getting is what you want in return for giving, the customer wants to know what *they* are going to Get." It's your marketing responsibility to tell them up-front what they are going to get. If they don't see or hear "what's in it for them" within 15 seconds, they will be responding immediately with a mental note, "Sorry, not interested!"

People are extremely busy and their lives are hectic. When they look through their mail, read a newspaper, listen to a telemarketer or hear a sales presentation, they are looking and listening for only two things: "Can I get what I want from you?" or "What's in it for me?" They are not going to dig through your sales letter, advertisement or your verbal presentation to find out if you have anything of interest for them. If you don't tell them immediately and up-front what you have for them, you will have lost them. That's why it's so important for you to know exactly what your prospects and customers want before you begin spending money on marketing. *Test, don't guess!*

Tell Them They Will Have To Act Quickly To "Get."

You do that with what is called a *Sense of Urgency*. Tell them the offer ends on a particular date, perhaps in a week or two. Or tell them that there is a limited supply, or that they will receive a special bonus if they act now, but they will miss the bonus if they put it off. Home Shopping Network, QVC and Groupon use a ticking clock to create urgency!

Tell Them the Details of What They Will "Get"

You have your prospect's attention with your headline by telling them that you have what they want. Now it's time to tell them *exactly* what they will get if they respond to your marketing offer. Also tell them exactly what is included. If you don't, it will come back to haunt you in the prospect wanting his money back.

The following Commandment #14 Call-To-Action applies here: Tell Them What They Must Do to "Get" It. Don't assume that your prospects and customers will figure out how to get what you are offering. They won't do your work for you.

Repeat yourself. Repetition is the Father of Understanding.

Tell them again what they will get! **Explain** how quickly they must act. **Instruct** them what they must do to "Get" it. It's always a good idea to re-cap your offer in a P.S. (postscript.) Very often, people will skip down to the P.S. right after reading the headline. By repeating all of the specifics of your offer there, you stand a much better chance of ensuring that your prospects will understand your offer. Tell them again what they will "get" if they respond by the deadline, and exactly what they must do. Now that you have repeated it, sum it all up in one sentence. Here's an example: P.S. Drop the enclosed post card in the mail by Monday, May 29th, to *join up* or *purchase* the product or service!

Conclusion: Getters don't get. Givers get! The companies that give get back in kind. The "Give to Get" marketing approach is relatively inexpensive when it comes to the cost to implement. It's powerful! It works! The real cost is the investment of time to discover and evaluate what your customer base would perceive to be *valuable information.* **Test not guess!** Once drafted, then every ten days send one of the four emails to your prospect base. "Strive not to be just a success, but rather to be of value." Albert Einstein

14th Commandment:
Thou shall Call-Customers-to-Action

I guarantee if you want to increase your sales lead-generation, you'll pay heed to this business commandment. What I'm going to share with you now will significantly increase your sales. If you're writing your own ads or an advertising agency is writing your ad copy, you must sit down and dissect the *Call-To-Action*. It is of paramount importance that the prospects know exactly what you want them do and what action step they should take. Ineffective advertising is always tainted with a weak *Call-To-Action*.

Advertising guru, Leo Burnett, conducted a research analysis of the ad campaigns that failed to see what they had in common. The first thing was that the ads and commercials didn't have a clear call-to-action. They were branding messages, not sales solicitations. The good news is that it's easy to fix by concentrating and testing various call-to actions. Too often, it's overlooked by thinking that the creative is the most important element. Wrong! It's just the opposite. It would be like designing the world's best phone book and not have the phone numbers for a customer to call.

The same holds true when you analyze direct-response Internet communications. Those with weak calls-to-action produce puny results. If you've been to a typical website design firm to build your site and the website doesn't have a clear, strong *Call-to-Action*, you have an online brochure which has virtually zero marketing effect. Website designers are basically a new breed of graphic designers and they are not marketing experts. That's why most websites don't make any money!

Burnett also found that his failed ads used many more adjectives than effective ads did. From a statistical standpoint, on average, ineffective ads used about 24% of the ad copy with adjectives, whereas successful "offer" campaigns had an adjective ratio in the single digits.

Example: "Read this book" is stronger than "Read this *amazing* book." In school, I remember learning the difference between a declarative sentence and an imperative one. The imperative told you exactly what to do and that's what I'm telling you to do. Strike as many adjectives as possible.

One of the most powerful calls-to-action was when President Ronald Reagan said, "Mr. Gorbachev, Tear Down This Wall". He didn't say "Mr. Gorbachev, Tear Down This *Terrible* Wall." See how an adjective would have taken the power out of that line? We didn't need to be told the wall was terrible; the facts spoke for themselves.

Nouns and verbs persuade and inspire. They are the DNA of your sales communications.

For example: Abraham Lincoln's Gettysburg Address only had 13% adjectives in a speech that only had 285 words. Or take Winston Churchill's famous rally speech, "We shall fight them on the beaches, We shall fight them in France, We shall fight them on the seas and oceans. We shall fight with growing strength. We shall defend our island no matter the cost." It's very clear what his rallying call-to-action was. Notice Churchill didn't say: We shall fight them on the beautiful beaches. We shall fight them in Gay Paree." That powerful speech had only 12.5% adjectives. It was nouns and verbs that inspired action.

When President John Kennedy said: "Ask not what your country can do for you, ask what you can do for your country," he didn't say what can you do for this beautiful country. He didn't say this amazing country. The point being, the adjective would have drained the power of the statement.

What do all these great speeches have in common? They are all great sales presentations.

They have clear-cut **Calls-to-Action**. They are written to persuade and inspire. It's facts and verbs that cause you to take action. So strip away as many adjectives as possible.

Also limit your use of graphics and pay more attention to copy. The Bible has no pictures, no photos, just lots of text. And it's the bestselling book of all time. Your web designer is not your prospect. He might love graphics, but copy is what sells. Copy allows you to start building a relationship with your reader, essential for having any chance of closing a sale.

Your home page should feature your main sales presentation. It should launch right in with an attention-getting headline. It should look exactly like a sales letter you might get in your mailbox except, instead of an order form and reply envelope, you'll have links or buttons that say: "Click Here to Order" that will take readers right to the order page and credit card form.

Internet Call-To-Action Mistakes

Because copy is needed to provide your prospects reasons and compelling arguments to respond to the call-to-action, let them read about what you offer. People search the internet for information (text), not graphics or pretty layouts, so give them the information they want in text format. People will read if they are interested. There are five Internet *call-to-action* mistakes I don't want you to commit:

Mistake #1: Requiring prospects to click a link rather than scroll to take action.

You never want a prospect have to make two calls-to-action before a buying decision can be made. When you ask them to click a link to buy, that's one commitment. The second is the decision to buy commitment. It's easier for readers to scroll than to click a link. Scrolling allows readers to hold their finger on a button and scan your headlines and subheads. If something grabs their interest, they can read it without clicking. Clicking and waiting for another page to load takes time. It's annoying to a prospect. It's a stopper, kind of like an intermission at a long movie or play, and the people leave.

The average time a surfer spends on a Website is about eight seconds. Don't waste time by making your reader click and wait to read. Put the entire article, your entire presentation on one page or more, even if your reader must scroll and scroll and scroll to read everything on the page and you have created a potential buyer

Mistake #2: No attention-getting headlines or subheads.

Headlines and subheads tell your scanners what all this text is about. Research shows that you have just eight seconds to grab your website visitors' interest. They don't call it "web-surfing" for nothing. If you don't grab your visitor's attention and break this pattern of behavior, then they will hit your site, stay for a few seconds and then they're gone. Usually forever.

So when they do hit your home-page, you need to present them with a clear and pressing reason to stay. And that means a headline. Don't let your website designer or your graphic artist sell you on the idea of logos, pretty pictures and whitespace. That's just a "brochure website." Trust me, they don't work. No one cares about your logo, the picture of the anonymous businessman in a suit at the top of the page, or empty space devoid of any meaning. Website designers are NOT marketing experts.

Mistake #3: Sending prospects to your corporate website.

You should never send a prospect generated by direct-response to your website; it will confuse them. On your website there's too much going on; rather you send them to a simple Landing Page that will focus only on the ordering process. The graphics on the Landing Page should be the same as those that appear in the DRTV commercial and in print. You want a familiarity look between the response device and the Landing Page. It insures the prospect that he/she is at the right place to order.

Mistake #4: You didn't Dash Flash!

When people type keywords into a search engine, they are looking for information. No one types "only show me sites with *Flash*" page introductions." In fact, if a searcher gets to your site and is greeted with an elaborate Flash presentation, half your visitors will leave your site before they ever get to your sales presentation. Search engines also hate "Flash" pages. Search engines are interested in content and in delivering information to searchers.

Although "Flash" is a detriment, a website Video Spokesperson is a powerful communication tool. The trick to maximizing the Spokesperson's effectiveness is to have the 3D Spokesperson begin to immediately speak when the viewer clicks on the website. The Spokesperson should appear no more than twenty seconds, having the role of a navigational guide. Another effective method is to have a video in a box on the home page and then the viewer has the choice to watch the video or not. Remember, you want the visitor to scroll.

Mistake #5: Selling many different products and services from one website.

It's not a good idea. Websites should be dedicated to selling one thing or one service, or asking your reader to take one, and only one, action (even if the only action is to read the article). If you sell many different products and services, you should have many different Websites dedicated to each product and service you sell. The reason is, when people search the internet with their keywords, they are looking for one and only one thing. They will buy from the website that is selling that one and only one thing because it appears to visitors that this is your area of specialty.

Narrow-casting has always been the gate to paradise in direct marketing. This is even more true in the age of the Internet, where people are looking for your service or product with highly-focused keyword searches.

The good news is making your website profitable can be achieved fast, as long as you stick to some simple, but very powerful, fundamentals. And you can start right now. It all starts with your Home Page, because that's the first thing people see when they hit your website.

The search engines want to make sure your website is in line with the keywords you've selected to include in your Meta Tags and with the keywords people are typing into search engines. What makes a search engine valuable is that it does a good job of taking searchers to websites that are exactly in line with their keyword searches. You want your site high on the list of search results listed for the keywords you're using to bring people to your site.

Two website tips to ensure that your "home page" passes the 8-second test:

1. **Killer Headlines**. You cannot make money in direct-response without "killer headlines" for your mailings, newsletters, advertisements and the website's Home Page. A headline is text, usually black, bold, and big, which gives your visitor a large, exciting and compelling promise that if he or she continues reading, you're going to give them some significant reward for doing so. If your headlines are fascinating, your readers won't mind reading on to get the details. If the headline of your ad is currently the name of

your company, you can almost certainly increase the response rate by changing the headline.

Headlines are what draw your readers into your copy. If your headlines are fascinating and intriguing, your readers won't mind reading on to get the details. *"Attention-getting"* headlines play a major role in the readership of PR releases. On average, five times as many people read the headlines as read the body copy. For a moment of levity I have written the following PR headlines that push the envelope and cause you to want to read on to know more:

> *Want Dope for College?* S.A.T Tutor

> *Surprise Dad, Have the Kids Shot.* Photographer

> *Going to Hooters For The Food* ? Sex Therapist

> *Today's Special : Spay or Neuter your Best Friend!* Veterinarian

> *If Your Kids are Continually Sniffling, Have Them Shot!* Flu Shot Doctor

> *Let Me Tell You All the Good Things President Obama is Doing!* Republican Flyer

> *How My 6-Yr.-Old Daughter's Lemonade Stand Made $750 in 2 Days* Financial Planner

> Free offers also make for good headlines, i.e. "Here's Your Free . . ." Call Now!

2. **AIDA Formula**. Structure your web page copy according to the AIDA format. The acronym AIDA stands for **A**ttention, **I**nterest, **D**esire and **A**ction. Follow this classic rule and you can't go too far wrong. Your home page should follow your headline and tell your "story." It's got to be interesting enough to keep them riveted to the page long enough to get them over that 8-second "hump."

- You get their **A**ttention with a strong, compelling headline offering them a clear benefit for reading further.
- Then you get their **I**nterest with strong opening paragraphs that spell out the problems they face and the benefits your product or service offers.
- You then fan the flames of their **D**esire by "twisting the knife" of their pain and really showing them how you can ease it and make their lives better.
- Finally, you get them to take **A**ction with a strong *Call-to-Action* on the homepage. The offer will normally be a free report, samples, discounts, video or any topic of interest to the visitor in exchange for them giving you their name and email address.

Every single page on your website should have a single purpose to justify its existence and should, therefore, follow the AIDA formula. It seems too simple and too good to be true, but it's used by the greatest copywriters and marketers simply because it plugs into our natural human psychology and it works!

Conclusion: You must test *Call-to-Actions*! You must test headlines! You must test! Test again! And test once more! When the wind takes the air out of your business sails it's best to test the oars. Find out what makes the cash register ring. It's worth the testing. One headline has been known to out-produce another headline by as much as 600%. That increase is with no change in the body of the letter at all! That means that a promotion which made $1,000 could have made as much as $6,000 just by changing the headline and powering up the *Call-to-Action*! "Never stop "testing" and your advertising will never stop improving." David Ogilvy.

15th Commandment:
How To Disarm the Nuclear Sales Bomb

The Disarming Formula I recommend is threefold: Objection Busting Questions + The Taoist Way + Sun Tzu's Flexibility = A Successful Disarmament. I bet no sales guru ever espoused that equation to you. Having owned a major advertising agency and a direct-response TV production company for more than 50 years, you can imagine how many sales presentations I have made and written. The veracity of the formula is that it is based on a diversified range of products. So let's begin.

First, you must develop an arsenal of *objection-handling questions*. In your quiver you must have twenty-five plus action arrows that you can draw upon to guide your sales presentation.

Second, adopt a Taoist Manner. What's a Taoist Demeanor? It's a state of harmony that prepares you for an upsetting, foreseeable event. That disruptive event may be the client dropping the "*Price Question Bomb*." Knowing that might occur, you need to prepare your mind with what Taoists call the inner smile. You're invincible if you are mentally smiling. Taoist is a calming philosophy originated in the Han Dynasty (203 BC). The reason why the Taoist Way needs to be part of the formula is because when the price question is asked or a challenge arises, it's human nature to get nervous or change demeanor. At that critical point, some sales people even lose confidence. The prospect isn't going to buy; he is not qualified or interested. Therefore, you must call on your inward smile to defuse the bomb!

Third, don't be rigid. 2,500 years ago, long before Napoleon Hill, an ancient Chinese general named Sun Tzu wrote a book called the Art of War. It has had a major influence not only on military thinking, but on business tactics. He won many battles without going to war. Analogy-wise, he believed that professional selling requires a skilled warrior, but that warrior need not go to battle to win. One of Sun Tzu's central principles is that rigid plans never work. Way too many times I have witnessed a sales trainer or a sales manager bellow: "Here are the 200 steps you must follow to be successful." They never talk about flexibility. Granted, you need to be skilled in sales techniques but, more importantly, you need to prepare to be flexible.

No military General will go into battle without a plan, nor should you. Even a military plan has a Plan B, a back-up plan. So should you. One of the most powerful objection-handling techniques is to *"Bring It Up Before it Comes Up."* By being flexible you can reverse-engineer your sales presentation to anticipate the objections that the prospect might bring up. You then can address the objections in the body of the sales presentation. I recommend you go to Amazon and get a copy of The Art of War by Gary Gagliardi, my Harvard Business School classmate. It's enlightening reading.

The Nuclear Bomb

In any sales presentation is the customer immediately asking you "What's the price"? That jolting question often comes in a variety of forms:

1. Give me a ballpark price. I won't hold you to it.
2. How much does something like that cost?
3. I'm a busy person; just give me a bottom-line price.
4. I don't want to talk about anything until you give me a price.
5. I asked you how much is it?

The price of your goods and services is always a primary concern to your prospects. Whether you like it or not, price is top of mind with the majority, if not all, of your prospects. You probably find the question of price comes up in your conversations with prospects long before you have had the opportunity to build value in your product and service.

The early introduction of the price question seems to put you in a position of having to choose between two rules of selling that appear to be anti-ethical to one another at this point. Always answer your prospect's questions honestly and directly, and *never* discuss price until you've built value in your product or service. Fortunately, you can honor both rules. The easiest way to handle the question is to give the prospect a direct answer and then bridge back to your investigation of their wants and needs to build value.

There are four ways to disarm the nuclear bomb question before it explodes in your face. Three of those ways are booby-traps that will sabotage your sales presentation. Let's examine each of these approaches. Tell the buyer . . .

1. That's a stupid question. If you don't want to know the value of what you're buying, you should get a new job and become a lifeguard in a car-wash.

    It might make you feel good, but it's not a good idea!
2. Ignore the question. That's a bad option. Plus, it's offensive.
3. Defer the answer until a later time. Doesn't usually work.
4. The best way to disarm the deadly bomb is to answer the question with what I call the *Bomb Squad* approach. This tack is to make the customer feel as if you have his interest at heart. Here are five proven approaches:

The *Helpful* Approach: We have a full range of prices based on what you're trying to accomplish. Let me help you narrow your choices and then we'll look at the price.

The *Permission Selling* Approach: I could give you a price, but it might be misleading. Allow me to ask a few questions to be sure I understand what you're trying to accomplish. Then, let's look at price. Is that ok?

The *Curiosity* Approach: I'm curious. We have a range of prices depending on the value, from low to high. You'll likely fall somewhere in between. Let's find out. I need to know exactly what you're trying to achieve and then we can select the right product and price for you needs.

***Like You, I Have a Job to Do* Approach:** It's my job to make sure you receive the greatest value. Don't use this approach; the buyer really isn't interested in your job.

The *Story-Telling* Approach: One of the most powerful ways to handle an objection is with a story. The reason why stories are so persuasive is they act as invisible selling. Stories also suspend time.

Identify true stories that address the objection. One way to start off the story is by saying "That reminds me of a story of a client who was in a similar situation. Let me tell you what he did." Tell a story about someone who resisted but, when the customer compared values, we won. That decision to compare resulted in a major cost-savings and a huge success for the company.

Tell a story that addresses their objection. EG: tell a story about a prospect that didn't get insurance because they wanted to think about it. Of course, an accident happened and they were screwed. They had the same "concern" as yours.

In each of the Disarming Response Approaches you have the opportunity to defer the answer until the *value* is established. You accomplished this without ruffling any feathers. Falling prey to answering the premature price question will give no value to your product. In the absence of value, whatever price you tell the buyer will be perceived as being too high.

The key to addressing the price question is understanding why the question is asked in the first place. Many salespeople see the price question as an objection; it isn't. It's an honest question by the prospect who is trying to determine their interest level in your product or service. Just as you are trying to qualify your prospect, they're trying to qualify your product or service as well as qualifying you, and one of the major qualification questions they have is price.

Again, you've given an honest answer to the price question since, at this point, you don't know what the package will cost. Instead of trying to answer an impossible question, you've given the typical cost range and then followed with a question that will put the conversation back on track of investigating your prospect's needs, allowing you to gather the information you need to build value in your product before you get into a serious price discussion.

Price questions need not create problems for you or for your prospect. Price is a natural concern for the prospect, but knowing a price without understanding the real value of the product or service is meaningless. You or you salespeople's job is to answer your prospect's question and return the conversation to a point where you can build value for your prospect, so they can appreciate the price in context of value. If you refuse to answer the price question, you run the risk of insulting or angering your prospect—not to mention the damage you do to your credibility and trustworthiness.

Price is not the only area where you need to prepare responses to challenging questions.

Your entire presentation should have navigational questions woven into its fabric. These *"Bridge Questions"* will help you to keep the prospect involved and focused on what you're saying. To Be the Best You Can Be, doesn't mean you have to join the Army; it means you're going to sit down at your computer and write 25+ *objection-handling* answers pertinent to your business. It's going to take you the better part of ninety minutes. Once written, say them aloud. Repeat the reading aloud for seven days. The goal is to make your responses sound like second nature. The average male salesperson is glib, personable and has a tendency to believe he knows what to say to get his way. That may be so, but the really-successful salesperson has his/her twenty plus objection responses at the top of his/her mind. The salesman who is prepared will, in the long run, be the better producer. I should mention that, in general terms, women are usually better prepared than their counter part.

Attesting to the importance of preparation, successful trial attorneys don't wing it, they have thought out each question they are going to be asked and the anticipated answer.

I encourage every salesperson to invest the time to sit down, analyze and then write out their twenty five objection-buster answers. Please invest the time. I'm here to help!

Be Cautious: Use the standard answers you find in *"How to Sell"* books as a guide only. You want to have twenty-five answers to objections, "customer-specific." I have listed a few responses as a start. Some are appropriate, some aren't. Look for the difference!

Objection: *I need to think about it.*
Response: We offer incentives for making a decision today.
Response: I understand. Other than thinking about it, I am sure that you have some other concerns, do you mind sharing those concerns with me?
Response: Simply say: "Tell me more."

Objection: *I need to talk to my wife.*
Response: I understand. So if your wife says "yes," does that mean that you will do it? (Trial close) Let him respond.

Response: Let me ask you another question, what if she says "no?"

Response: If the decision was up to you, would you move forward today?

Objection: *Price is too high.*

Response: We don't negotiate prices, company policy. However, we do offer incentives for moving forward today.

Objection: *The price is too high.*

Response: Actually, one of the biggest benefits of the program is the price and here's why. Who wants to stay in the cheapest hotel?   (Bad answer, 1980ish, it's stale)

Objection: *The price is too high.*

Response: By too high, what exactly do you mean?
                                        (Bad answer, 1980ish, it's stale)

Response: How much too much is it? (Bad answer, 1980ish, it's stale)

Response: Compared to what?

Objection: *I don't have the time.*

Response: Other than time, is there anything else that is preventing you from moving forward?

Response: When will you have the time?

Response: Tell me more about that.

Objection: *I don't have the money.*

Response: I can appreciate that. Other than the money, is there anything else that is preventing you from taking action today? (Ask a closing question & be silent).

Response: I'm sure you have other concerns than money?

Objection: *I have a bid from another company.*

Response: Without comparing what we have to offer, how do you know if you're getting a real value? Isn't that so? Comparing is a real value to you.

Very Important: You also need to store *Bridge Questions* in your arsenal. For example: The customer is persistent in wanting to know the price of the truck he is interested in purchasing. You answer him directly: "It's $22,842" followed by the bridge question. "Will you be pulling a trailer often, or just on occasion?" You've answered your prospect's question, but you have led him back into a discussion of about what he wants and what he needs. With that information, you or your salesperson can now highlight the features of the truck that will meet those needs and the benefits of those features that will give value to the price of the truck. Questioned answered. Price value established!

In a software example, the price has been given and the *Bridge Question* that follows might be something like: "Well Keith, although I've given you a general price range, installation and training of the software can be anywhere from a few thousand dollars on up. By the way, what other applications do you run that our software will have to be integrated with?"

Our clients have found the following 9 keys helpful in successfully negotiating a price that is higher than that of their competitors, even in situations where it appears that the only thing that matters to your counterpart is a low price.

1. **Ask great questions.** Sales people who lack confidence tend to ask closed-ended questions that yield short answers with little information. Control the conversation by asking great questions that uncover a customer's true needs and the importance of value to them in this negotiation. Ask those great twenty-five, open-ended questions, then listen.
2. **The Taoist Way.** The inner smile will build your confidence. Part of the reason your product or service is worth more is because of the service and support you and your team provide. If you don't believe that your product or service is worth more, then it will be difficult to convince a customer that paying more than your competitor's price is a good thing.
3. **Develop a positive vision.** You have to believe that you are going to win this sale, and that it is going to be in the customer's best interest that you do so. If you feel you are going to lose on price, you already have. Get excited about putting together a plan with options, that will lead to a successful outcome. This one may be tough, but you have to believe in a positive outcome. An important part of your positive vision is

to remember that you have more price power than you think. If the client still returns your phone calls and emails, or agrees to meet with you, you have power. If you have no power, they would simply place the order with the competitor at a lower price.

4. **Deal only with the organ grinder.** Make sure you are dealing with the decision maker. If price is going to be the deal-maker or breaker, there is no sense dealing with the monkey when the organ grinder is sitting in the next office.

5. **Understand the true needs of your buyer.** There are two types of needs: Explicit needs like price, quantity, quality, features, terms, warranty and delivery. Then there are implicit needs like the buyer's reputation, credibility, and need to look good to their boss and peers. Implicit needs almost always override explicit needs in determining the outcome of a negotiation. If implicit needs did not override explicit needs, we would all be driving YUGOs, the lowest-priced car ever sold in the United States. If the thought of buying the lowest-priced product would impact your station in life and social image you would gladly pay the higher price. Price is a function of perceived value.

6. **Commit to Sun Tzu Philosophy. Be Flexible.** People hate giving up value! Everyone hates to pay a high price but they hate giving up value even more. Don't ever lower your price without taking away some value at the same time. If you lower the price, but don't adjust the value, the customer will continue to ask for an even lower price.

7. **Sun Tzu "Know your enemy/competition better than your customer."** If you don't know your competition, then you tend to take anything your buyer says about your competitor as true. To successfully defend a higher price, you need to know your competitors and you need to know the truth. Do your research in advance; not being the best-prepared undermines the value of your higher price.

8. **Sun Tzu "Don't be rigid."** Develop options. When it comes to selling at a higher price, options help to change the buyer's question to "*How* will they use us?" not "*If* they will use us." By

adjusting price and value and developing a variety of options, you will find it easier to defend a higher price.

9. **Sell the Problem, not the Solution.** Almost always, there is a reason for your higher price. Most salespeople try to sell the solutions of their product or service. It is much easier to defend a higher price by selling the problem. If you buy the lowest priced back-up system and it fails in a catastrophe, what impact is that going to have on you and your company?

Conclusion: I encourage you to set forth a *bomb-squad mentality* to diffuse the price bomb. The best way to handle objections is through prevention. Treat the cause, not the symptom. You won't win them all but, with these 9 strategies, you will win a lot more price wars. Start celebrating your success!

16th Commandment:
Thou Shall Negotiate With Your Ears.

Your ears, not your tongue, play a major role in successful negotiations. Your ears will never get you in trouble. Hear and you will know their vulnerabilities. Speak and you'll know at least one person is listening.

There is a difference between handling tough sales questions and the art of negotiation. Negotiation, in the classic diplomatic sense, assumes that the parties are more anxious to agree than to disagree. It's a chess match. It takes a whole different skill set.

In the previous commandment, "How to Disarm the Nuclear Bomb," I wrote about the necessity of having 25+ objection-handling questions in your quiver and the importance of practicing the art of asking questions. The same is true when negotiating, but there are three other components that need to be blended with the prepared questions: Listening, Researching and Win/Win. Listening plays a major role in negotiations. The late management guru, Peter Drucker, said "Professional listening is critical to closing a deal." Drucker was also quoted as saying: "My greatest strength as a consultant was to be ignorant, ask a string of questions and punctuate them with silence."

In the world of negotiation, it has been well known that silence can be a powerful tactic in helping you achieve your negotiation goals. In fact, a lot has been written about when it comes to agreeing to a deal point or making a concession, such as: the first person who talks loses. We are not in agreement with this point in every silence situation. Sometimes, it may be in your best interest to speak first if the deal point holds little value in the overall negotiation and allows you to focus on the significant points of the deal. What's critical is that you remember when you do open your mouth and break the silence, stay focused and make sure that your words help you achieve your goal.

The benefits of silence are powerful in the world of negotiation. You get time to think before you respond. Since a lot of people don't like silence, you may create pressure for your counterpart to respond first or concede. By listening, you create a feeling in your counterpart that you care about them and value their opinion. It's my sales philosophy: *People like you much better when they do the talking.* Most importantly, silence can increase your chances of achieving your sales goal.

Here are five tips that will help you to use *Silence* to achieve your negotiation goals. Silence is the euphemism for listening.

1. The art of listening is comprised of four steps: Ask, Listen, Think and Rephrase. Ask your question. Then Listen. Even though you know the answer, think for a few seconds before you respond. Rephrase the prospect's answer to show that you have listened. For example: a.) "Let's see if I understand . . ." b.) "I understand what you said, would you consider . . . c.) "Am I correct in understanding that you said . . ." Don't say 'What you're trying to say is . . .' It implies the customer is an idiot and can't say what he means. Also, avoid "What I hear you saying is . . ." It's overused.

2. Make sure your client or customer understands the question you're asking. Mis-communication often occurs when you're not clear and the other person is not paying attention. That's another reason you have to test your twenty-five navigational questions for clarity of understanding. Here's a good example of not understanding the question: A blonde walks into a bank and says, "I'm here to speak to the loan arranger." He's not here. "Well then, can I talk to Tonto?" Make sure you know what you're asking and, equally important, is that you understand what you're being asked.

3. When you negotiate, never ask a question that you don't know the answer to. A great example of the consequences for violating that rule of selling/negotiating was when O.J. Simpson was asked at trial to try on a glove. Prosecuting Attorney, Christopher Darden, had foolishly asked a question that he didn't know the answer to. When the glove didn't fit Johnny Cochran countered with "If it doesn't fit, you must acquit."

4. Take notes. When you ask a question to confirm a deal point or gain a concession, shut-up and listen. If your counterpart is silent, look down at your note pad and write down the question you just asked. By the time you jot down the question, you can look up and most likely, your counterpart is going to break the silence.

5. Regularly rephrase and verify what the opponent has said. This is an important part of active listening, because it helps you to avoid misunderstandings. On ambiguous points, ask your opponent to spell out exactly what is meant. You can challenge some questions by saying something like: "I don't really think that's the right, would you explain your point?"

6. Question. Can you restate in terms of . . ." This may cause your customer to change the question and put it in a form that you're willing to deal with.

Although you may have heard the negotiating axiom: *He who speaks first, loses.* Take a page out of Sun Tzu book: don't be rigid, break the silence if needed. It is important to know that you can be the one to break the silence contest and not concede anything. Example: I'm in New York City making a major presentation to a Wall Street Firm. The key decision-maker and I must have read the same book on the Art of Negotiation and he and I entered into a silence contest. Minutes passed, no one spoke! We stared at each other. Board members squirmed with uneasiness. Then it dawned on me if I break the silence with laughter and say you win, I will not have conceded anything except the loss of the contest. When I laughed aloud, he did too. If you are the one who needs to break the silence, do so by asking a question that changes the direction.

Many times Marketing Executives don't put the art of negotiating into their sales training. Gerard Nierenberg, the author of the first formal book on negotiation, *The Art of Negotiating*, explains it this way: "When two or more people exchange ideas with the intent of changing the relationship in some way, they are in negotiation." When it comes to the prospect-seller negotiation arena, you need to negotiate in a way that will ensure a win-win outcome, one that meets the needs and goals of both counterparts and makes both of them willing to come back to the bargaining table to negotiate with each other again at a later time.

Winning takes place before negotiations take place. If you're going to be an effective negotiator, you have five *need-to-knows* in advance. Preparation wins every time!

First, you need to know what is *not* negotiable.

Second, you need to know what concessions you will be willing to concede.

Third, before any negotiation begins, spend time walking in the shoes of the other side. Write down the points you believe they will argue.

Fourth, you need to know what you hope to accomplish.

Fifth, you need to know all you can about the company, the decision-maker, and especially what he wants to accomplish by participating in this negotiation.

I've been involved in many negotiations in my long career. They were all different in some ways and alike in others. But through them all, I've identified four "platinum rules" to be the most helpful in closing a sale or negotiating a deal. Why platinum? Well, the golden rule is "Treat people like you want to be treated." The platinum rule is "Treat people like *they* want to be treated." To find how they want to be treated, you need to do some research. Usually the face of the company is the profile of its buyers or principals. Before any negotiation begins, understand the interest and positions of the other side. Mentally walk in their shoes. Plus, you have to know all about your competitors. Not knowing decreases your success by a multiple of two.

Early in my career, I was quite often burnt for not knowing what the competition was offering. I would end up competing against myself. It was also brought to my attention that I was making too many concessions too early in the negotiations. People don't appreciate concessions that they get too easily. They tend to assume that they really aren't worth much. My advice to you is always sell your concessions.

Although I was winning, I was leaving money on the table and my competitive spirit was alienating the people I was negotiating against. I wasn't allowing all parties to walk away with heads held high. Despite my intentions to do otherwise, my mistakes kept recurring. To correct these business faux pas, I bought a journal and after each negotiation session I would write the negotiation or sales presentation mistakes I had made. It was the right prescription. I recommend that you journal. I still have that old tattered journal. Now and then I open the book and smile at how far I have come from those brash, *thinking I knew it all* days.

Here are some of the notes I have underlined in my journal:

I want to clarify the very popular term, your *"walk away price"* as being your lowest price. It's the most you're willing to concede. When you're bargained out, make the final offer and let the other side walk if they don't want it. But you should never be the side that walks away first. Even though you have made your final offer, stay at the negotiating table. An agreement may come to fruition. I'm an eternal optimist. I'm willing to wait at the table!

On page 10 of my journal, I underlined this pearl of wisdom in red. Remember, some of the best deals you will ever make are the ones you did not make. All of us have contemplated buying something from an individual, or entering into a business relationship with a company, and just getting a gut feeling that we should say "no." So we have walked away from the deal. Later, when we heard negative information about this individual or company, the information reinforced the fact that we had made a great decision. In negotiations, your head may try to rationalize deal points to make your gut feel more comfortable. Remember to go with your gut instinct, many times your head, over-rationalizes. Robert Heller said it best "Never ignore a gut feeling, but never believe it's enough!"

On another page I wrote: Don't negotiate against yourself. This is especially true if you don't fully know the position of the other side. Much is learned if I just listen. I need to wait until I understand which points are more important to the other side.

Within the journal there were three more "don'ts" that were circled in red:

Don't underestimate your power. The other side wouldn't be negotiating if they didn't want something you have.

Don't be intimidated by status. There is as much danger from having a *"little-shot"* complex as a *"big-shot* complex."

Don't be bamboozled by statistics. It's a new world out there and the statistics from yesterday may not be meaningful.

I have found that there is an art to Compromising. Compromise is difficult because both sides are usually reluctant to back down from their original stance. Remember, people hate giving up value! Everyone hates to pay a high price but they hate giving up value even more. Don't ever lower your price without taking away some value at the same time. If you lower the price but don't adjust the value, the customer will continue to ask for an even lower price. Over the years I have seen top negotiators use five "compromise tactics" that result in win/win situations:

1. *"Sweetening the Deal"* is a tactic used extensively in business to make a deal work, but this tactic only works if you have decided in advance what the sweeteners are to be.

2. The *"If . . . then tactic"* seeks a compromise based on mutual agreement, meaning if you could agree to a counterpart's stance, would they concede a part of their stance and accept your proposal? For example, you might say: "If I agree to do this, then are you willing to do that?"

   For example, when a buyer balks at a price or condition, the seller should counter with something like: "Of course, that comes with a full, three-year warranty at no extra cost and we'll even throw in the delivery for free." Don't lower the price!

3. *"Guarantee It."* Don't cut your prices; instead, increase your value. One of the easiest ways to increase your value, especially when your prospects are particularly nervous and fearful, is to offer a really powerful, unconditional guarantee. So when you eliminate the risk by offering a guarantee, you're doing something very powerful. It means all the risk of the sale going wrong is transferred to the seller. This, by itself, gives the buyer a massive confidence boost. His or her investment is secure. He/she can't lose.

   Here's an interesting fact: The longer in time you make your "guarantee" and the more wide-ranging it is, fewer customers will ever contact you for a refund. If the guarantee offer is a 30-day guarantee, by the time day twenty-one arrives and they're not sure, they'll come back for their money. But if that guarantee is, say twelve months, the customer relaxes and you don't get called on the guarantee. It seems to be a quirk of human psychology, but it's there nevertheless.

If you have a reliable product, don't be concerned with the number of people taking you up on your guarantee. It's a pure numbers game. If someone asks for their money back once in every fifty sales and you're making an extra one-hundred sales a week because of your guarantee, you'll make a fortune.

4. *"Trade-Off Concession."* Effective negotiators aim to never concede a deal point without getting something in return. Concede small. If you're going to concede and lower your price in the opening round of the concessions, concede small. Your first concession sets the stage for all future rounds of concessions.

5. *"Differentiate or Die."* If everything is truly apples to apples and there is zero difference between you and your competitor, then you are right. The only thing that will differentiate you is a lower price. When your counterpart continues to talk with you about price, they are telling you that you have something of implicit value to them other than price, listen, Listen to what they may be saying!

Recognize that people seldom buy things solely based on price. If it were really true, we would all be driving YUGOs and the YUGO car company would still be in business.

Although the entire auto industry is in a world of hurt trying to sell based on price incentives, over the last 18 months it became obvious that sometimes people are unwilling to buy even when you lower your prices to well-below your costs. The positive example is that most cars are bought not because of their price, but because of the implicit needs they meet for the buyer. Many a car salesperson has closed the deal by simply saying: "You look really good in that ride . . . people will notice!" Remember, a Porsche is not a car; it's a status symbol. Focusing on the value that your product provides for the customer rather than boasting low prices will give you a competitive advantage. Do price wars work? You might have a fighting chance if you are Wal-Mart, Target or Amazon. For the rest of us, it's a losing battle. So use those compromise tactics and win.

When nothing else works, use humor. Humor has a way of uniting even the most diverse of people. It is extraordinary in its way of producing paradigm shifts. It pays to use humor as a strategy to mitigate conflict. Used wisely, there really is no better way to illustrate a point in your quest for honest and effective communication. Remember Commandment #11: Thou Shall Know That He Who Laughs . . . . Lasts.

Conclusion:

During the negotiation, your opponent will be probing for your vulnerabilities. A wise man will know where he will be attacked. Therefore, know yourself. Just as important is for you to know all you can about the other person's company, know all you can about the decision-maker himself, and especially what he wants to accomplish by participating in this negotiation. If you're going to be an effective negotiator, you have five *need to knows* in advance. Winning takes place before negotiations take place! If he's a good negotiator, he will ask you questions that you may not want to answer this early in the negotiations. So don't allow him to start first; you should strive to come off the block first in order to control the beginning of the negotiation.

The art of listening is comprised of four steps: Listen, Ask, Think and Rephrase. It's your navigational wheelhouse. Ask your question. Then Listen. Even though you know the answer, think for a few seconds before you respond. If he queries back; pause, think and rephrase his answer to your question in your favor to show that you were listening. Look the person in the eye. Remember what your parents said when you were a kid: "Look at me when I'm talking to you." People see you are listening when you are looking at them.

Don't underestimate your power. The other side wouldn't be negotiating if they didn't want something you have. Preparation wins every time.

17th Commandment:
Thou Shall Not Cold Call

Persistence without horse sense is not profitable. To make two-hundred cold-calls to get two leads is a waste of time. Sun Tzu, in his book "The Art of War," philosophizes: "An army is like a fire. It will burn itself out." Cold-calling will burn out your sales force. In this, the *Age of Information* with so many direct-response marketing resources, there is no reason to cold-call. Besides, cold-calling destroys your status as a business equal. One of the things I have learned along the way is that, in order to be supremely successful, you need to project a strong image of success. Cold-calling, if not done right, creates the perception that you're trying to scrape up business. It comes off as needy and desperate.

All of us would rather have a person buy our product than having to resort to selling them. Buying is the willing acquiring, for money, something that you want or need. The buyer generally leaves the transaction feeling happy and satisfied. On the other hand, selling is attempting to convince another that they need your product or services, despite the fact that they may not. The purchaser typically leaves the transaction with a strong feeling of Buyer's Remorse.

In my experience, I've come to the conclusion that cold-calling definitely equates to my definition of selling, which is the task of convincing a person they need the product or service. On the other hand, using leverage systems to attract qualified prospects to your cause is my definition of buying. In a cold-call scenario, a potential prospect receives an "out of the blue," a cold-call from a person they don't know. After some coercion on the part of the salesperson, an appointment is granted.

When the first appointment takes place, the prospect is automatically resistant because they naturally assume a high-pressure sales presentation will take place. They are on guard. Let's say the customer makes the decision to buy, paperwork is signed, and installation of delivery is scheduled. The customer can't help but wonder if they might have gotten a better deal elsewhere and that they should've called around instead of buying from someone who walked in off the street.

It's obvious that a negative apprehension will follow through the entire selling process. By contrast, let's take a look at the same series of events constituting my definition of buying. The customer is contacted by one of the many methods being employed by the salesperson, the customer recognizes the product or service as advertised as something they happen to need and the customer makes the initial call. The customer's frame of mind is set at this time in a positive mode.

Now, let's look at a more down-to-earth example of why I believe that persistence is not profitable, other than the fact that Sun Tzu said so: If you have a *"buying"* customer, you'll probably close the deal on the first or second appointment, whereas those customers who have been cold called require, on average, four calls or appointments to close a deal. It has been shown that the revenue from sales resulting from cold-calling will be significantly less when compared to a buying scenario. Here's the problem: If 65% of a salesperson's time is used for cold-calling, it doesn't equate to time well spent. By only dealing with the customers who bought on the first or second appointment and writing off the ones who did not, he can easily double his income because he has more time soliciting qualified buyers.

Way too often, I hear this irrational argument: Internet marketing is expensive, direct mail is costly, TV and Radio are too pricey. My only option is cold-calling. Wrong, so wrong. There is Mobile-Marketing, Affiliate Marketing Programs, Biz Texting, QR Bar Codes, Social Media and Event Sampling that will create a buying mentality. Basically, you can't afford not to employ one or more of those new lead-generators. The increase in sales will more than pay for the media generators. To be successful in this economy, you need to change from cold-calling selling to relationship building with the new sales tools.

If your business is totally dependent on telemarketing, I would replace cold-calling with what I call a *Knowledge Call*. A *KC* is one in which the telemarketer has done enough research about the prospect and the decision-maker that the call can no longer be considered a cold call. The "getting to know you" research that I'm recommending you have your people do isn't difficult, but it can be time consuming. I'm warning you in advance that you'll be tested. They will be challenging you, saying that they don't have time to do the research to make their calls. There will be no complaining once the approach generates more money than before. And it will!

While telephone sales might be a numbers game, it isn't really about the number of calls so much as it is about the number of quality *KC* calls. I'm not naïeve in thinking that in some boiler rooms the telemarketer companies can't know anything about who they are calling because dialers are used. But when the telemarketer can acquire knowledge, he/she should do so because it will dramatically increase the closing rate.

The Horns of a Dilemma

A marketing debate rages between *KC*-calling vs. Social media. One side says: *KC*-calling is more effective than social media. The other side will counter with: Social networking is faster. Counter point: No, it takes longer to narrow-down qualified targets and messaging them one by one can take forever. After you send your messages to them, you might wait hours for an answer (if you get any responses at all). Social marketing is more personal than calling a stranger. Not so. When you get a person on the phone, you have their attention. The debate goes on: Twitter, Facebook and Linkedin are where today's action is. With *KC*-calling, you can reach around 30 people an hour and get *yes* or *no* answers from all of them. Mobile-Marketing can reach a thousand or more people in an hour.

The *Horns of the Dilemma* continues. Some say social media is still a very poor way of getting new people interested in your business, but it does have its place. It's a very good way to maintain existing relationships with people that you've already done business with. It's certainly not, however, the end-all, be-all of marketing. I'm convinced that Twitter's 140 characters will not be sufficient to have a buyer call back. The exception would be if you had a free offer or a recognizable major discount.

The issue: Is *KC*-calling more effective than social media-marketing? The answer lies in understanding the differences. *KC*-calling's purpose is not to build relationships or establish communities. It's to sell or get an appointment. Whereas the social media platform builds and retains relationships.

When the goal is to set an appointment, *KC*-calling is not a tool for selling. It's a research tool that you can use to find qualified prospects who have an interest in your product. It's important not to sell on the phone, but rather to increase the value of the meeting! Ask discovery questions to find a compatibility and discover their pain. Take just enough time to determine interest so that you can set up a face-to-face meeting. It's at this meeting when the real sale happens.

You're not impaled on the "*horns of the dilemma debate*" when you understand that neither cold-calling nor social networking are truly effective without prior *Knowledge*. If the telemarketer's role is to set an appointment, the only way that's going to be accomplished is if the salesperson has prior *Knowledge* of the prospect's business and needs. Without *Knowledge* you perpetuate a square-circle: the prospect doesn't know you and you don't know the prospect's business. It doesn't matter if you use Twitter, Facebook, or a Megaphone outside their office; you're going to hear: "Not interested!" followed by the deafening sound of the hang-up.

There are seven mistakes that will prevent you from making a *Knowledge Call*:

1. You or your telemarketers are not doing any research prior to each *KC* being made.
2. You begin your conversation by saying how great your product or service is, rather than uncovering solutions for the pain the prospect is experiencing. To acquire that information, the tone of the conversation is one of caring. The questions are engaging, but not intrusive. This is an art. Skillful questioning has to be learned and practiced. Once the pain is discovered, your product becomes the solution and people buy solutions!
3. You're not talking to the monkey-grinder. You're "monkeying" around with the gatekeeper.
4. You are obsessive and compulsive in making as many cold-calls as possible, rather than just making a few, qualified *KC* calls.
5. You are not using contact management software like ACT! or Salesforce.com.
6. You are talking more than listening. Yakkity Yak.

7. V.I.P. You're not sounding like the Energizer Bunny. The euphemism is you don't have the Eye of the Tiger. If you're not excited, why should the prospects be interested? To booster your confidence, research shows that you would be shocked to discover how little prospects actually know about a company or what they have to offer. Be confident. People, especially 'early-adopters' and genuine 'switchables,' love to learn something new.

Setting Appointments

Cold-Calling differs from *KC*-calling appointment setting per se, because you will know about the company's needs and how you can solve their problems. You're no longer a telemarketer, but a valuable resource. Even in wildly-successful programs, most prospects will decline your request to meet with them. A rough rule of thumb I use is that you can expect to book a meeting with one out of every eight decision-makers you speak to. Seven of eight will decline. That doesn't mean there isn't great potential business among those seven. It just means that they don't know you. If you don't have a solid "Plan B", you won't have a chance to get their business.

Plan B is a continual buyer educational program. On a routine basis, the prospect receives current information about your company. There's a great song from the musical *My Fair Lady* that sums up Plan B: "Getting to know you, Getting to know all about you, Getting to like you, Getting to hope you like me."

If you are making major sales which involve large sums of money, have longer sales cycles or ones to which your prospects only add/switch vendors every few years. The odds of initially getting them on the phone at exactly the right time are low. You need a "Plan B" to automatically communicate with viable prospects cost-effectively and without you having to make numerous phone calls in the hopes that you catch them at the right time.

Plan B enables you to educate people as to new options that will help them, options they had not previously been willing to consider because they have been on the receiving end of your Plan B strategy. I have seen a lot of business generated from prospects whose response to an initial offer is a resounding "NO" as a result of effective plan B strategies.

Plan B enables you to realize a high return on investment on your prospecting activities as you will be able to generate business from those who don't immediately agree to meet by enabling them to "raise their hands" when they are ready to buy. We all know that the best prospect is the one who calls you! When someone says *no* to your prepared *Knowledge Call,* I recommend you immediately counter with something like this: "That's fine. But I have something that you might be interested in receiving. It's a free (insert whatever you are giving away free)," followed by a comment something like "This has proven popular with executives in your position. May I put you on that list? You can opt-out anytime." Three times out of four the answer is "OK".

Because you asked permission to send material, the prospect who has said "no" is now saying "yes." You now have permission to send them your collateral material. Don't waste that permission by sending information that's of little value. (Review commandment # 12). To create trust, the valuable collateral must be delivered in multiple hits over a period of time which builds trust, credibility and awakens them to consider options they had not previously considered.

Plan B requires you do three simple action steps:

1. Enter their e-mail address into your web-based, sequenced e-mail program and they get all your messages automatically, without you having to think about it.
2. Code the e-mails appropriately in your Contact Manager Program. ACT and Goldmine seem to be the most popular. Both work well. A code is entered which indicates the size of the potential opportunity and a code is entered which indicates the step in the prospecting process. Simple, easy, and it enables you to focus your time and money where it will do the most good.
3. Schedule a call back once you feel that the prospect knows your product's benefits, is fully informed of what value you can deliver, and has formed an impression as to your worth and credibility. Don't let more than seven days go by before making the follow-up call.

You'll find that this is a very different conversation. This is a much warmer conversation than the initial *KC*-call. I have noticed two things: First, people are much more likely to take or return your calls. It makes sense as you are now perceived as a valued service provider, even an expert, not a dreaded vendor. Second, people open up about their needs and challenges once they trust you. This is important as it enables you to properly code them and properly allocate your future time and resources.

Conclusion:

There is a fundamental marketing and sales principle that has held true since the beginning of time. People buy when they are ready to buy, not when you are ready to sell. This does not mean that prospects will never buy from you. In fact, a study by the Gartner Group showed that 87% of prospects that inquire about a product will purchase it or a similar product within twelve months. Why leave your sales to chance? Staying in front of your prospects is the single easiest way to boost sales and grow quickly. Your job is to stay in front of them with Plan B elements: valuable information mailings; PR exposures; free trials; biz-texting and Groupon offers in exchange for their contact information. If you're not there, someone else is going to land that business.

Today's leads are tomorrow's buyers. To really grow your sales, you need to fill your funnel with prospects so you can convert them into buyers down the road.

18th Commandment:
Thou Shall Not Look Through a Keyhole With A Glass Eye.

Many years ago, Peter Drucker wrote and spoke these strong words: "If you want it, measure it. If you can't measure it, forget it." Why is that axiom so potent? The reason is, if you can't measure it, you *can't manage* it. The essence of management is to make knowledge productive and that's accomplished by measurements." Without a gauge, it's like a glass eye looking through a keyhole. You're blinded to knowing how well or how bad your business is doing. What gets measured gets done; what gets rewarded gets done repeatedly. Ponder what Aristotle said, "We are what we repeatedly do."

It's having a keen eye for the obvious to state that measurements are a necessary management tool but what's not so obvious is that measurements are a great motivational tool. Let me ask you a question: do all the people in your company know how well they've done before they go home? It's been proven that employees who know how well they are doing will do well. People need measurements to excel.

Bowlers are a good example. How many people would bowl if they hung a sheet over the pins so they couldn't see how they did on every roll? Answer, no one. Unfortunately, this situation is similar to how many companies work. The sheet must be lifted and the score must be recorded so a person will feel good and excel, to do better. Sidebar: The Y generation workforce wouldn't be too interested in working for an organization where their contributions aren't measured.

Equally important: if you're going to be successful, you must also consistently monitor and measure your customer-satisfaction status. If

18th Commandment:
Thou Shall Not Look Through a Keyhole With A Glass Eye.

you don't know your Website Ratios, you're *blind* to online advertising effectiveness. I would estimate that well over 85% of website owners don't know their website ratios. When I meet with a new client, I always ask the owner and the Marketing Director to tell me what their website ratios are so I can help them make informed business decisions. Too many times there's a blank look like a deer caught in the headlights. I'm going to ask you, Do you know your website ratios? Great if you do. But if you're like most and don't know, let me share what you need to know: Online advertising is a math science. Web ratios will tell you if your advertising dollar is effective and giving you the best ROI.

The four Web Ratios you need to know are:

1. Average cost per visitor.
2. Average cost per prospect.
   Someone who hasn't bought yet.
   but has given name and email address.
3. Average cost per customer or client.
   Even if you're not selling per se online and
   just generating leads, over time you'll know
   how many prospects turn into clients.
4. Average value per visitor.

Now, for more detail . . .

Your ***average cost per visitor*** is what you spend, on average, over time to get visitors to your website. For example, if you get 1000 visitors to your website in a month and you have spent, let's say $200, your average cost per visitor for this source is $ .20 ($200/1,000). Over time, you'll use different methods or sources to drive traffic to your website. You'll want to track each one separately.

Your ***average cost per prospect*** is what you spend, on average, over time to get a prospect to "opt-in," and give you their name and e-mail address. Tying into the above example, if you gathered 100 names and e-mail addresses during the month (Note that this is a 10% opt-in rate—100 prospects/1,000 visitors), your average cost per prospect is $2 ($200/100 prospects).

Why is this important? If you effectively use an email follow-up system, you'll turn prospects into customers over time. You have to know what you're spending to get someone to become a prospect.

Your ***average cost per customer or client*** is what you spend, on average, over time to get someone to become a customer or client. Let's say you're selling something from your website; again, tying into the above example: if during the month you get 10 customers (Note, this is a 1% sales conversion rate: 10 customers/1,000 visitors), your cost per customer is $20 ($200/10 customers).

Why is this important? You need to know as soon as possible if you have a "problem" with your website. Here's an example: if you've budgeted 10% of your selling price for marketing and advertising, and you're spending 20%, you have a problem. For example, using the above numbers, if your selling price was $100 and you had budgeted $10 (10%) to get a customer, you'd be spending $20 or 20% and that's a problem.

The last ratio, ***your average value per visitor***, is just what it says. It's the average value of every visitor that comes to your website, whether or not they buy. This ties your selling price and your sales conversion together.

In the above example, if your selling price was $100 with 10 orders, you'd have $1,000 in revenue. Your average value per visitor would be $1 (10 x $100/1,000 If you can obtain a visitor value (average value per visitor) of $1, you're doing well.

Look at how the first and last numbers tie together. You're investing (Note, I didn't say spending) now that you have your numbers. $ .20 to get a visitor to your website and every visitor that comes is worth $1; that's a 5 to 1 return on your investment. There's a lot more detail about your ratios once you get up and running, but this should give you a good feel for why these numbers are important.

Here are three suggestions for driving traffic to one's website:

Begin by contacting other webmasters for a possible link-exchange partnership. The key is locating websites that are relative to one's own website. Contact them and make a link-exchange. *Link or Sink*!

The second way is through writing one's own articles. This is an effective way to promote a website because good content that is appreciated by readers will lead them to visit the writer's very own website out of sheer interest.

The third way is through joint-venture marketing. This is one of the most effective ways of promoting a product or a service. Having a partner through ad swap or link exchange is beneficial to both parties as it allows them to reach a wide customer base in a short amount of time.

Here I go again, *Link or Sink*!

The key to internet success is linkage. Link your company's information into your social media network (LinkedIn—Facebook—Twitter). Link your news into applicable blogs. Most importantly, establish an Affiliate program. The concept of Affiliate Marketing is simple: affiliates promote your website and you give them commission on the sales they generate or the click-through they send. The most popular model, by far, is giving affiliates some form of commission on the actual sales they generate on your site. This is known as *performance-based marketing.*

The ways in which an affiliate promotes your site can vary dramatically, from simply adding a text link or banner on their site pointing to yours all the way to having specific pages on their site detailing your products or services and linking directly to them on your site. It's also possible for affiliates to promote your web site offline with posters, flyers, etc, and still track their commission.

The difficult part is accurately tracking all of the visitors and sales that the affiliate sends. This is known as *affiliate tracking.* I would recommend that the person joins an affiliate network, where the network provides the affiliate tracking. Every time an affiliate links to your website, the network's software tracks which affiliate is responsible for sending the visitor. The affiliate tracking is also tied in with your ordering system, so that it knows if a visitor sent by an affiliate makes a purchase.

Studies show that, before new customers buy, it takes four to eight contacts. Once heard, the mind races; eight contacts seems to me to be a jealous mistress of my time. It would mean that I would have to commit more time than I have. Not true, the time savior is an auto-responder. A multi auto-responder is a program that allows you to send out multiple e-mails over a certain period of time. The work is automatically done for you.

N.B. Is your website as good as you think it is? Do you believe that your website is at its peak efficiency in converting visitors to prospects? Why guess how effective the site's content and design is in converting your visitors? Oh, I can hear what you're thinking: "This is going to cost me more money to make my site better. I have already spent X number of dollars on the site." The good news is: What I'm going to recommend is free!

It's *Google's Website Optimizer,* a free website testing and optimization tool, which allows you to increase the value of your existing websites and traffic without spending a cent. Using Website Optimizer to test and optimize site content and design, you can quickly and easily increase revenue and ROI whether you're new to marketing or an expert.

Conclusion:

Without a gauge it's like a glass eye looking through a keyhole. You're blinded to knowing how well or how bad your business is doing. It's of paramount importance that you know your web ratios. Test, don't guess, otherwise you will confuse probability with profitability. Measurements are a necessary management tool. But, what's not so obvious is that measurements per se are a great motivational tool. People need measurements to excel.

19th Commandment:
Thou Shall Generate Word-Of-Mouse

It used to be just Word-of-Mouth; now it's *Word-of-Mouse*. When was the last time you used the Yellow Pages Book? Who do you know who recently bought an Encyclopedia Britannica? If you want information, you let the *mouse-do-the-walking*. Today the mouse is the big cheese when it comes to PR.

In this era of relationships, a brand is a *Dialogue*. You have to engage your customer in a conversation about the merits of your brand and get their opinions. The goal is to turn the dialogue into a testimonial. Whether you're a small, local business or an online giant, the basic dynamic doesn't shift. Happy customers will always bring in new customers. It's my opinion that PR is still the best and most effective form of creating a dialogue. There are two drivers that make a PR campaign successful: testimonials and more testimonials. "90% of consumers trust peer recommendations."—*Neilson Global Online Consumer Survey.*

Conventional PR	*Word of Mouse PR*
Email	Texting
Radio	Social Media
Television	YouTube
Newspapers	Blogs
Events	Organic SEO
Announcements	Twitter
Print	APPS

Word-of-Mouth is now *Word-of-Mouse*. The internet is today's testimonial generator. Agencies manufacturing PR releases and campaigns is an era gone by. Releases are not drafted by companies

151

and sent out; rather they emanate from the bottom-up. The genesis now is customer satisfaction, two-way dialogue and transparent communications.

* Identifying the people most likely to share their opinions
* Studying how, where and when opinions are being shared
• Providing the tools to make it easier to share information

Who are the people most likely to talk about you? Those who I call the *Influencers*. You know them; the person who always has the best recommendation for restaurants, new drinks, music, books, whatever they are passionate about. They have a potpourri of information that they believe will be valuable to their friends. In short, *Influencers* are a personality type, not a person. They represent about 15% of the North American population. Influencers have three distinct personality traits: 1. They are always searching for new things. *Word of Mouse* is the best way to get to this group. 2. They share information with their friends by communicating with stories. That's a heads-up; your PR copy should be story-driven in a newsy way. To Influencers, great stories are social currency. They thrive on being at the center of their social circles and are constantly searching for new ways to increase their collection of stories. They do this by finding new information and sharing it in an entertaining way.

From this *Word-of-Mouse* process, brands gain awareness and credibility. The Influencers' status continues to grow as their friends try the brands recommended to them and report back with positive feedback. As the positive feedback grows, the *Influencers* become more vested in the brand's success.

To ensure success, you must "let the mouse do the walking" (a little play on Yellow Pages' slogan "let your fingers do the walking"). You want to tap the tweet, harness social media and boost the buzz.

Although the delivery of PR information has broadened, the drafting of press releases remains tried and true. Like any news story, the purpose is to provide your readers with current information that will catch the searching eye of the Influencers. Here are the key copy essentials:

Headline. **VIP:** I recommend you have at least two headlines: One headline that is aimed at capturing the attention of the Influencers and the other headline needs to evoke the interest of potential customers.

People read only what they are interested in. A prospect is very myopic. They only want to know how reading the release can be a benefit. Example: One of my clients was a company that wanted to introduce a revolutionary medical device to help men suffering from urinary incontinence. Tough challenge, wouldn't you agree? A pure medical copy release will be of no interest to the Influencers. Therefore, we had to create a name for the product that would be of story-telling interest. The product was named Gee Whiz! The headline was "Gee Whiz Makes Adult Diapers Obsolete."

To capture the interest of potential customers, the headline needed to be benefit-oriented: "Gee Whiz Debuts a Revolutionary Treatment of Male Urinary Incontinence" and the other headline was "Medicare Covers Gee Whiz Treatment of Male Urinary Incontinence."

New search engines have very specific headline limits of what they will display: Google—60 characters; Yahoo—120 characters; PRWeb—170 characters. Below the Headline is the *Dateline,* where the City, State, Source, Day, Month and Year appear, followed by the body of the release.

DON'T WE, WE. We do this . . . . **We** do that . . . . Did I tell you **We** also do this . . . ? Stop the We,We. When a person is reading a PR release they only want news; the body content tone is natural and objective like a news story, not like an advertisement. As you were taught in school, the opening paragraph is the most important. The same holds true for a press release. You want to make sure that the opening copy covers all the benefits. Ideally, the length of the opening paragraph is 25 words or less. The total length of the release should be between 300-400 words. Using the example of the GeeWhiz release, the copy reads as follows:

"GeeWhiz (*http://www.urinedevice.com/index.htm*) introduces a revolutionary health-care product, giving men suffering from urinary incontinence a cutting-edge option for eliminating embarrassment. It makes bulky, adult diapers obsolete. Even better, Medicare covers the cost of the GeeWhiz product." TIP: Include no more than one link per 100 words of your release. These links include both anchor text links and active URL hyperlinks.

What Not To Do:

* Do not refer to yourself or your company as "I" or "We" It's a red flag!
* Avoid clichés like "customers save money" or "great customer service!"
* Do not use exclamation points or hyperbolic claims like "Amazing Service!"

The Word-of-Mouse Difference.

Marketing's role has not changed. It's still about defining target markets, writing benefit-oriented copy and providing unparalleled customer service but the techniques that were successful in the past will be less and less effective in the future. Marketing to the Social Web is not about you getting your story out; it's about nurturing relationships and dialoguing with customers and prospects. In the Social Web sales environment, your brand's success is based on the dialogue you have with your clients, customers and prospects. The stronger the dialogue, the stronger the brand; the weaker the dialogue, the weaker the brand.

James Cameron's name selection for his movie, Avatar, was right on target because it fostered dialogue. People wanted to know what Avatar meant. With knowledge comes sales. A good example of wanting to know more was when, at the World Cup in South Africa, the world heard the dull, monotonous sound of droning bumble bees. The Web World was buzzing with people wanting to know what was causing that sound. When the bloggers explained that it was a long trumpet-shaped air horn, the next question was: "What's it called"? "Vuvuzela". "How do you pronounce it? How do you spell Vuvuzela"?

For a moment, clear your mind of all those traditional, one-sided communication techniques while you participate in this evaluation guide. You'll rate your transition modality on a scale of **1 to 5,** 5 being right on the money; 3, you have some understanding; 1, you don't have a clue. Sprinkled into the following questions are the *old-fashioned building blocks* that must be present for a company to be successful.

1. Rate how effective the conveyance of your Unique [ ]
   Selling Proposition (USP) is to the social media and your
   website.

   (What's a USP? *Unique Selling Proposition.* If you didn't
   know, subtract 1 point)

2. Have you created an environment that encourages [ ]
   user-generated content?

3. Do you have plans to use QR bar codes and Google mega [ ]
   tags in your marketing mix?

4. The New York Times says "*Texting is the most powerful* [ ]
   data-gather."

   Agree?

5. What is a texting Short Code? Are you familiar with its [ ]
   business applications?

6. Do you have plans for your marketing mix to have a [ ]
   consumer voting strategy?

   The importance of five-star reviews by experts and
   reputable organizations have given way to consumers
   voting for everything from cruise lines to cookware.

7. Viral marketing is word-of-mouse over which you have [ ]
   no control. Have you developed a policy and a plan to
   control negative online reviews?

8. Do you have an *elevator pitch* that promotes a dialogue [ ]
   with the web viewer?

9. Are you into blogosphere investigations to understand [ ]
   what's happening?

   It's of paramount importance that you understand what
   the bloggers, the analysts and consumers are saying about
   the industry, your competitors and your company.

10. To what degree are you familiar with *Technorati*, a search [ ]
    engine that searches blogs to find exactly what you want
    to know and need to know?

11. Would you consider a *consumer bottoms-up* marketing mix [ ]
    strategy?

12. Ford Motor Company's strategy of using the American [ ]
    Idol contestants in their TV commercials was brilliant! It
    fostered an online dialogue that resulted in sales with the
    younger market segment. Have you and your ad agency
    begun to explore similar strategies?

    Total   [ ]

Add up your numbers. If you scored 60, you lied. The majority of
the entrepreneurs and company decision-makers who have taken this
evaluation guide scored in the range of 38-43. Scoring in that range
means only one thing: you haven't learned how to "let the mouse do
the walking" for you.

Lots of people say that in the world of social media it's your job
to engage with customers. You have to talk to them, be accessible
and give them something about yourself to hold on to. I guess that's
true. However, I think businesses have to go even further than that. I
think, if you want customers to evangelize your brand and be loyal to
you, you have to do more than just talk to them—you have to woo
them. You have to make your customers swoon. As a small business
owner, how can you get customers to swoon? Here are 11 practical
suggestions:

1. **Monitor the social networks for people talking about your
   company.** When they're saying positive things, say "thank
   you." Very few executives say "thank you." Do so because good
   reviews will continue. When it's negative, get more details and
   then say "thank you." When they're asking questions, answer
   them and say "thank you." When you find people talking
   about your company, respond and ask them to further voice
   their opinions via the social media.

2. **Show up places they wouldn't expect.** Your customers have
   certain places where they hang out on the Web, besides Twitter,
   Linkedin and Facebook. Find their local watering holes and be
   there when they need you. Don't hijack their conversation or
   try to sell your services; just be part of their world and let them
   know you're there.

3. **Create a blog and write content designed to address customers' problems.** Check your site logs, customer e-mails and/or complaint section to identify your customers' biggest issues, problems, and concerns. Write content that will take these issues away. Solving someone's problem and making them look good is the best way to make them fall in love with you. Women have known this for years.

4. **Plant small surprises.** Whether it's a surprise like creating a "thanks for commenting" page or becoming involved with a charity, sending a small gift included with their order, or chocolates sent on their birthday, offer a small gesture that your customers wouldn't expect. Let your word of mouse rock their world and tie that unexpected experience into their perception of your brand.

5. **Start relevant conversations.** Whether it's on your blog, a social media site like Facebook, or in a competitors' Forum, start conversations with qualified experts about topics relevant to your customers. Don't use these conversations to sell; just share your advice and act as a helpful member of society. If your customers want to know more about how you can help them, they'll know how to get in touch with you.

6. **Guest Post on their favorite blogs.** You love golf and you get really excited when you find other people who love golf. Why? Because you feel an instant connection with them because you already have something in common. Guest Post on your audience's favorite blogs and show them you love their favorite blogs as much as they do. Word of Mouse will create an affinity that never existed before.

7. **Admit you don't know everything.** Woo your customers by asking them questions. Hold polls. Ask for constant feedback. Invite customers in and make them part of your sales process.

8. **Be responsive.** When someone takes the time to e-mail you, have your Word-of-Mouse leave a comment or respond in a timely manner.

9. **Write for your audience, not for the search engines.** The search engines may bring you traffic, but they don't bring you

customers. To find customers, you need to solve their problems and give them something they can use. That's what your content should focus on, not on what's popular or what search the engines want you to write about.

10. **Make your blog and website accessible and easy to navigate.** Don't make your customers feel stupid. They'll leave.

11. **Build your own network, but don't lose sight of your core readers.** Go out and build your small business. Grow your network, create relationships and network your way into powerful partnerships but don't lose sight of the people you're trying to reach. They are your core. These people are the ones who at the end of the day, matter most to your business. Those are eleven proven ways I think businesses can woo customers and make them loyal to your brand. Add to these ways to the ones that have worked for your company.

Conclusion:

The Mouse is the pen of the Future. What hasn't changed is the work needed to define the target markets and the investment of time to write the benefit-oriented copy, but the style of the copy has changed. It's like the line from the T.V. show *Dragnet*, where sergeant Friday would say "Just the facts, maam, just the facts." PR web readers want just the facts.

Marketing to the Social Web is not about you getting your story out; it's about nurturing relationships and dialoguing with customers and prospects. Press releases are an important way for organizations to share information with their audience, but too often executives' quotes are throwaways. You know the ones I mean: with executives saying "How pleased they are about a new partnership" or "How excited they are to be selected for a project." Who cares? Well, certainly not the Y generation.

Make sure you wean your PR agency off using old phases like these: "For all intent and purposes," "In real time" (A decade ago it was cool; now with the world so connected, it's no longer a defining benefit); "Thinking outside the box" (a cliché that doesn't die); "Nice" (Blah); "Great" (Blah); "Marvelous" (Blah) . . . Blah, Blah. There are many more, but the point has been made. It's the era of innovative Buzz.

Papyrus releases, air-wave interviews and trade journal articles will always be with us, but now there is a 600-lb. Gorilla named Web in the press room and it needs to fed in the ways I have set forth in this commandment. It can be summed up in three (3) words: News, News & more News.

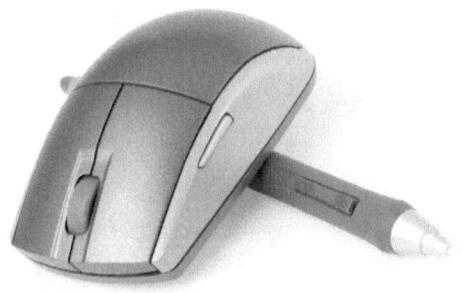

20th Commandment:
Thou Shall Not Blame Thyself for Not Being Able To Dribble A Football

This is a self-evaluation commandment. I'll guarantee that you are a violator to some degree. There are two types of executives who violate this most precious of business commandments. There is the person who has an overwhelming sense of personal infallibility. The other is the perfectionist. The *Infallible* one believes he will solve the problem & overcome the hurdles if he works harder and harder. In his infallible mind, he knows he can teach the cow to trot. He drives his fellow workers with tasks of futility. Unfortunately, over 50 years I have seen that overbearing person hurt his/her company. Instead of wasting time trying to make the crab walk straight, test and find out if there are enough customers out there who would buy a crab that could walk straight. Linear thinkers have a tendency not to place profitability as their number priority. Their myopic focus is also detrimental in that their subordinates are fearful of telling the naked king that his mental wardrobe should be changed.

The good news is: cows may never trot, crabs may never walk straight, but people can change for the better. It's all about attitude. Just as important as *owning a word* is having a good word for others and for yourself. Too many times, I have seen companies tread their way into a business purgatory because the leader hasn't a "good-word attitude."

The most deleterious of quirky personalities are the *Perfectionists*. They drive themselves and others crazy. Footballs weren't designed to be "dribbled." Unfortunately, it never occurs to a perfectionist that they can't dribble a football. Perfectionists strive to achieve goals that are beyond the reach of mere mortals. They take good qualities like drive, ambition, high standards and cleanliness and turn them into possessed passion. Their pursuit of excellence turns into an unattainable quest for perfection. This crazed mentality always ends in frustration, disappointment and failure.

Whenever a *Perfectionist* tries to relax, there is always a haunting voice that says *"work late", "clean the garage", "shampoo the rugs"* and *"tote that barge"*. Most are plagued by lack of joy; their humor has been allowed to atrophy for lack of use.

Perfectionists find it difficult to laugh about their imperfections because they either have none or they have so many that it's not funny. When someone is out of touch with their sense of humor, everyone around them suffers. Freud said that *"Laughter is the release of tension."* A third-century Roman writer named Lactantius said, *"Anything pleasant easily persuades."* Interesting, centuries ago the secret of being persuasive was linked to likability. If you want to persuade prospects and customers to buy, persuade investment bankers to invest, persuade philanthropists to give, persuade employees to succeed, you must have an aura of likeability. As a leader, it's your responsibility to nurture a pleasant experience environment for customers and employees alike.

Here's a Commandment-breaker that I have heard on too many occasions, *"I don't have to be liked or pleasant; all I have to do is deliver a quality product."* So wrong! There are no best products! Marketing is not a battle of products; it's a battle of perceptions. It doesn't matter if you have the best product. What matters is how the consumer perceives you. Marketing is a manipulation of those perceptions.

A recent major behavioral study shows that 63% of all dysfunctional families have one dominant *Perfectionist* in the family. Because *Perfectionists* have a difficult time putting themselves in other people's shoes, over time their personalities become crusted with the inability to be tolerant of family members and business associates. When you want someone to change, there is more self-love than love. Change comes from within; you can't impose your will and expect that someone will change. It doesn't happen that way. All you accomplish is making people resentful toward you. I just heard that little voice in your mind say: "If I lighten-up, it will only get worse. I'm the boss and that's the way I manage. If they want their jobs, then they'll do it my way. I'm not tolerant of imperfection." Isn't that interesting . . . now you're the person who won't change and try something new.

Pause for a moment and contemplate the role reversal that has just taken place. The person who you wanted to change can't force you to change any more successfully than you could pressure that person to change their behavior. This clearly illustrates, beyond any doubt that the power to change only comes from within. A new mentoring attitude on your part will make people want to change from within. It will amaze you! Over the years I have found that the biggest win is when people are sharing a common goal. People work together better when they are in the same boat.

Blaming and berating are the two things a perfectionist does to perfection.

Unfortunately, it causes an "emotional quake" that will register at least a 7.8 on the family Richter Scale. Marriage bells will crack, personalities will shatter and children will be lost.

Everyone who reads this commandment thinks it applies to someone else; certainly not to them. The truth of the matter is: this commandment applies to all of us in various degrees.

Are you a *Perfectionist* to a sinful degree? Here's how to tell: read the question/statement and then circle the numerical answer/response that is the *most truthful*.

		Yes	Quite often	Never
1.	Are you openly *critical* if it isn't done right?	3	2	1

		Yes	May be	Never
2.	Do you have a tendency to *blame* if things don't go your way ?	3	2	1

		Yes	May be	No Stress
3.	Do the people closest to you think you are too uptight, too stressed out and should lighten up?	3	2	1

Ask them. If you don't want
to ask them, it's a tell-tale
sign
you're a developing
Perfectionist.

		Dumb	*Don't listen*	*Not on Time*
4.	What angers you the most: people who do dumb things, individuals who don't listen to what you say, or people who are not on time?	3	2	1

		Told *No One*	Said *Sorry Once*	Said *Sorry Often*
5.	In the last 6 months I have *not* told anyone I'm sorry for what I have done or failed to do. Be truthful.	3	2	1

		Yes	*Kind Of*	*No*
6.	During that same time period, have you over scheduled your life and had to break a promise to a loved one?	3	2	1

		Yes	*Kind of*	*No*
7.	In business situations do you get upset quicker than you should and you know it?	3	2	1

		Frequently	*Sometimes*	*Not Often*
8.	Do you have a tendency to go to extremes in your work? Do you worry if you're doing a good-enough job?	3	2	1

		Yes	*Some times*	*No*
9.	Must it be perfect before you act? Do you spend too much time making it perfect?	3	2	1

		Yes	*At times*	*No*
10.	Do you feel isolated, yet superior, in your business?	3	2	

		Yes	*At times*	*Not really*
11.	Do you feel that you can do most everything better than your friends and loved ones?	3	2	1

		Angry	*Upset*	*Accept Criticism*
12.	If someone were to criticize you, what would be your emotional reaction?	3	2	1

Add up the numerical values you circled. If you have scored:

36-30	You are a "Possessed Perfectionist."
29-27	You are on the way to being one.
26-23	Time to make some changes.
22-13	You have it under control.
12	You're perfect, but you lied.

If you have just discovered that you have *Perfectionist* tendencies, here's a prescription for the predicament: the decision to be less of a *Perfectionist* is a personal one; no one can make it for you. It is something you must choose to do. Here are 4 tips that will help you begin to enrich your life:

1. Don't equate "giving up" with "switching." If you want to dribble something, *switch* to a basketball. Too many times a perfectionist has a hard time in adapting to a *new* sport (a new attitude). It has nothing to do with the person's business skills; the football was not designed to be dribbled. It will cast aspersions on the person's executive acumen when he/she is not willing to surrender and put their creative energies into a new ball game. Just because a ball is round it doesn't mean it will bounce (bowling ball, hockey puck and a baseball). It's not a sin to set a new course.

2. If your ship isn't sailing well and you're consistently experiencing dashed hopes, dismal dates, devastating results and disappointing progress, don't try to change the wind; change your course. You have control over the direction of your ship and no control over the wind. Don't fight it; use it. Even though Tiger Woods is one of the greatest golfers in the world, he has only 85% control of the game. The remaining 15% he has no control over. It's comprised of high winds, tall rough, wet greens, rock-hard sand traps, mosquitoes, deep divots and whatever else Mother Nature puts before him. Tiger has taught himself not to be concerned with the things he has no control over. Therefore, he only focuses on what he can control. Similarly, successful entrepreneurs have to learn to do the same and only concentrate on what they can control. That doesn't mean you don't sweat the small stuff if it's something you can control.

3. Try to empathize before you criticize. How do you do that? Simple. Just before you react, think for a moment about the person's feelings first, rather than their deed! Criticizing, accusations and placing blame only make people defensive. You never get your point across by being critical. "A gentle answer quiets anger, but a harsh one stirs it up." (Prov. 15:1)

4. You must immediately *burn the bible according to "should."* The word "*should*" is blasphemy. The greatest psychological sin you can commit is when you *should* on yourself and others.

Until you can do the entire New York Times Sunday Crossword Puzzle with an ink pen, don't waste your time trying to change people. You cannot make others be what you wish them to be since you cannot make yourself as you wish to be. You can't change others but you can change yourself. It's in your best interest to stop telling associates and family members continually what they should or should not do! "*Shoulding*" and teaching are totally different. When you *should* on someone, that person doesn't want to listen to what you have to say. Psychologists believe that there's a good chance they will repeat the same behavior. The only way you're going to win is for you to take on the demeanor of a teacher. If you take the mentor approach, it's guaranteed that they will listen!

Conclusion: Research studies show that Perfectionists are many times deleterious to the growth of a company. They have a tendency to stop learning, thinking they can solve the challenges better than anyone else. A Perfectionist's pride is expensive. The biggest problem is Perfectionists lose the perspective of time as they get more and more mired in details. They often miss market opportunities. There is an old New England saying, "While you're making the perfect pie, the hungry customer has gone down the street to another store and spent his money."

Aim at success, not perfection. Be a hard worker rather than a Perfectionist. Never stop learning from others. Give up your right to be wrong, because then you will lose the ability to learn new things. Say to yourself: "I will do my best and that will be enough!"

21th Commandment:
Thou Shall Expose Yourself Frequently

The more exposure to the public you have, the more your name becomes a powerful brand-of-choice . . . and you'll earn millions. *Personal Branding* can grow your business, increase your income and enrich your life. Why is that so? Branding oneself is one of the sure-fire ways to have consumers come to you, rather than you hustling them for business.

This is the era of relationships. When *YOU* become the *Brand-of-Choice* you represent a level of quality, consistency and trust that makes your customers' buying decisions far less uncertain and stressful. Because of *personal branding*, consumers believe that they know you and can rely on your brand to deliver the expected level of reliability, quality and performance. It's all about relationships.

Becoming known requires publicity. Frequent exposure to your customer base will, in a very short time, position you as an authority. In their minds, you become the marketing maven who cares! The power of PR lies in its inherent ability to position you as an expert, someone who can answer their questions. PR can take you from seller to expert. When potential buyers have a problem, they look for an expert to help them. In today's world, that means they search for a solution online and then check out the website for evidence of expertise. So what does an expert look like?

It can take many forms, but it almost always includes social proof (awards, certifications, or testimonials) and high-value, educational resources (like reports and presentations). When you publish this type of content on your website, you become an "expert" in the eyes of your prospects. In your quest for becoming a local business celebrity, the most effective exposure will typically come from mainstream media such as television, radio, newspaper and the Internet. Public speaking and publishing a book are also excellent ways to become an authority. In this commandment I'll give you the ways to become that local business celebrity. No matter the size of the company, a person who is positioned as an expert will be interviewed, looked-up-to and invited to speak.

When it comes to broadcast PR, the most-frequently-asked question is: "How difficult is it to be interviewed on television or radio?" It is not difficult if you have a quiver of great "hooks" that would be of interest to talk-show producers. They are called "hooks" because they "hook" the reader or viewer to tuning in. (e.g.: Why widows wear stilettos on the next Oprah! Montel: Sushi lovers stay tuned, find out if there's a Sashimi meltdown. Coming up next, Freakonomics will answer the question: Why do drug dealers still live with their mothers?

By giving them a good "hook" for a show or story that can be done around you, you're much more likely to get publicity. The absolute best way to get publicity is to give the media a "timely hook." The media wants to write or talk about what is happening right now. I guarantee you'll get major publicity if you read the breaking news on *USA Today's* website. Look for a story that you can tie-in with. If you find one, immediately send out a press release or e-mail pitch to your local (and even national) media, offering yourself as available for interviews. Trust me, if you do this throughout the year, big publicity hits will come your way.

I'll give you an outrageous example of the PR clout of a "*timely hook*": There was this dentist who had developed an incredible 30-minute tooth whitener. He had clinical results and oodles of testimonials, but couldn't get interviewed until he came up with this "hook." It was election time and his "hook" was that he could determine who were going to win the elections by looking at the candidates' teeth. The telephone rang off the hook with producers wanting to book him. During his interviews he was always able to weave into the conversation information about his tooth-whitener. You can do the same. Just *think-outside-the-box*.

What Producers Look For: The number-one thing on a Producer's list of what to look for in a guest is a guest who has self-confidence and can interact with others. Next, Producers look for guests with a decent screen appearance or a pleasing voice that projects well. Talk Shows also like to have guests who have watched the show and know what to expect. Producers favor guests who have a connection with a topic that's in the news. People who have written books on popular subjects are a virtual shoe-in.

What Are the Chances of Getting On a Show? As discussed, if you have timely "hooks" the chances of getting on a talk show are extremely good when you consider that there are 3,368 national and local radio and television talk shows on the air every day in the U.S. (another 2,339 if you include Canada and other English-speaking countries). It's good to keep tabs on these shows, along with what kinds of guests and topics they're booking. That way you know what to expect from certain shows and how to look and act for each one.

How to Contact a Talk Show: Keep a few things in mind when you contact a talk show. Producers have pet peeves. Don't call five minutes before air time to see if they received your packet. Also, make sure the recording on your answering machine sounds coherent. It's also good to practice a short spiel that you can deliver should a Producer call to test your knowledge in a qualifying pre-interview. People who are considered experts and can answer questions easily, at a moment's notice, get top priority.

Promoting YOU as the Brand-of-Choice

It's not conceit to position yourself as an expert; it's smart business. People will listen to what you have to say. Look what *personal branding* has done for these executives: Flamboyant Sir Richard Branson (Virgin Atlantic Airlines) and legendary Herb Kelleher (Southwest Airlines) gave a personality to their airlines, earning them millions of dollars. Donald Trump is the epitome of *personal branding*. As diversified in personalities as Steve Jobs, Simon Cowell, Lee Iaocca, Kiyosaki and Suzie Orman are, they were all of the same mindset: to make themselves the personification of their business endeavors from "unknowns" to "knowns," which has resulted in making millions for their companies. V.I.P. You don't have be the CEO of a major corporation to make *YOU the Brand-of-Choice."* Being a local business celebrity is easily attainable if you're willing to expose yourself frequently to the press.

Don't limit your exposure to just print and broadcast; consider tying yourself into the company's publicity promotions. Let me share a story with you that illustrates this point. Bloomingdale's (NYC) agreed to a weekend test of my client's industry's first—non-smear lipstick. This was a big deal. Bloomingdale's, on 59th St. in New York, is the worldwide queen of perfumes and women's cosmetics. If you get excellent sales results in Bloomingdale's, it is a passport to other major department stores. Being a small business owner, this was a great opportunity but she had a limited advertising, *pull-through* budget. So here's where *Event PR* came into play. The product was called English Ideas and the client was from England. Here's what we did. We rented every English Beefeater costume in New York City, totaling seventeen; hired seventeen actors to wear the Beefeater outfits. Each were given X number of product hand-out coupons to women. We positioned fourteen of them at the exit of midtown subway stations. Three were stationed at the Bloomingdale's entrances. The word got out to the television stations that there was an invasion of Beefeaters. Two TV stations sent crews to find out what was happening. When the store was at its busiest, my client made an entrance followed by seventeen Beefeaters in costume. The result was her being interviewed on two TV nightly news shows and the product being written up in several beauty magazines. Overnight, she became a lipstick expert.

Using PR as a Direct Response Tool

The Delahaye Study that audited the PR expectations of corporate America showed that well-planned, well-executed PR strategies could deliver ROI up to eight times the initial investment, not based on clippings or message consistency but on sales. So, how do you create PR activities that deliver real and measurable value for your business? How do you turn PR into a direct-response channel? Here are a few tips to get started:

Make them an offer they can't refuse. You will turn your PR into a measurable Direct-Response tool if you include an attractive offer in your release. Besides the offer, make sure the press release has a call-to-action.

Make them have an opportunity to hear from an Expert. Provide them with a way to contact the expert to gain information or have a question answered. The expert needs to be perceived as someone who understands their pain. They want reassurance, strong and confident leadership, and someone they can believe in and trust.

Make them know you know who they are. Consider who you are targeting with a particular PR message or activity, what you want that target audience to do and whether your message, value proposition and/or request are unique in the marketplace.

Make sure you isolate how you track PR from other marketing measurement efforts. Do everything you can to isolate the performance of your PR activity from other marketing activities in the same market, via the same channels or to the same audience. That way, you know that any activity on the part of your target audience can likely be linked to your public relations efforts.

Public relations is one of the most-leveraged opportunities in a marketer's toolbox, primarily because it has the ability to drive significant credibility, momentum, influence and thought-leadership for any company. The fact that it can also be more directly measured on an ROI basis should make stronger investments in PR even easier for everyone.

Promoting Yourself From the Podium

Business owners can position themselves as the knowledgeable expert in their profession by speaking to local groups. Here are seven "Dos" you should definitely Do!

- **#1. Find a Group**. Look in the classified ads of your newspaper or the phonebook business pages and you'll find dozens of references to groups that meet on a regular basis. Find the names of the presidents of organizations whose members are likely to want your products or services. Call the president and present a brief overview of your topic, then ask for the name and phone number of the Program Director. Almost all organizations are in need of interesting speakers for their meetings. For example, the Rotary Club, Real Estate Brokers, Bankers, Kiwanis, Marketing and Consulting Associations, etc.

- **#2. Write a Script**. Put together a half-dozen 15-30 minute talks, all related in one way or another to your area of expertise and go for it. Don't prepare a speech based on your sales pitch or you'll do more harm than good for your reputation. When you address the group, do not talk about selling them anything. They'll think you're just advertising and you don't want to do that. Talk instead about what they can do to improve some aspect of their lives or increase their sales.

#3. Say What the Audience Wants to Hear. Customize your presentation to the group, even if you use a standard outline. Arrive early and meet as many people as you can. Garnish the information you hear. We recommend that you use those sound bytes you heard to personalize your speech.

#4. Have a Clock in Your Head. Your talks should never be longer than 15-30 minutes, including a question-and-answer period. The group's Program Chairman will tell you how much time you have. These meetings are usually at noon and eating is more important than listening for most people there, so make it exciting and short. Limit your speech to three major points, smile, be enthusiastic, avoid pacing as you speak and focus on the audience's needs, not on your nervousness.

#5. Offer a Free Microbook. A Microbook is an electronic booklet that can be e-mailed to the attendees if they would like to know more about XYZ. Don't have your booklet with you at the meeting, but make sure that you get as many E-mail addresses as possible. It's also advisable to have a handout of the basic points of your speech. Make sure you place your name and contact information on every page.

Conclusion:

"Hooks" are the roots of publicity. It is not difficult to get press or be interviewed if you have a quiver of timely *Hooks* that would be of interest to publishers and talk-show producers. Let me explain what I mean by a quiver of *Hooks*. You must have at least seven marketing arrows that you can fire at Publishers and Producers with targeted *Hooks* regarding your release or interview. It's a work in progress.

The brand called YOU will give your products and services a voice. It will speak about reliability and believability. The more your voice is heard, the more Program Directors and Reporters will want an interview. It becomes Viral!

Be gregarious with the press It will pay great dividends. Be exposed to every PR and photo opportunity possible and it will generate favorable media coverage for your company. Be interesting and not commercial. Remember, mainstream media is only interested in NEWS!!!

A professional Public Relations firm will be able to create those opportunities. But let's say right now you can't afford a PR agency. It doesn't matter. This is not brain surgery. You can create and find those PR and photo opportunities on your own. The important thing here is that you develop a positive mindset that *YOU are the Brand-of-Choice*.

Many times small business owners come up to me and say "I heard what you said about exposing yourself to PR opportunities, but I'm not one who likes to be in the spotlight." My response is "That's fine. You must be true to yourself but I encourage you to give it a try because, in today's Business World to be successful, you must stand out from the crowd. The brand called YOU can't move up if you don't stand out. It's so much easier than you think. Bottom line: YOU basically need to become a Purple Cow. (See Commandment #6).

Remember, media professionals are crying out for good material to fill their papers and magazines and for conducing radio & TV interviews. With that confidence in mind, don't be bashful about adding a direct-response offer in your press release and broadcast interviews.

22nd Commandment:
Thou Shall Not
Fly on Kitty Hawk Airlines

You'll never get your company off the ground if you fly Kitty Hawk Airlines. Their marketing engines are old and so are the pilots. They cannot fly high enough for you to see the "*Blue Oceans.*"

The best advertising flight plan is *Direct Response*. It's a medium that can be tracked at retail, online and through the use of 800 numbers in TV or print ads. With the right analytics in place, you can act swiftly to take advantage of media opportunities aimed at optimizing sales in a very short time frame.

If your Direct-Response ads are not producing the ROI you need, it's easy to recalibrate the front and back-end offers and make the *Call-to-Action* even more pronounced. It will help lift the plane to profitability.

Direct Response offers the unique ability to stay in touch with the pulse of the consumer. Consumers are ultimately the control tower to a product's success. Avoiding an open line of communication in this era of relationships is a recipe for a crash.

Kitty Hawk Airlines can't thrive if they rely on the *New Marketing* to do their *Old Marketing* for them. Nor can the Super Sonics survive without the traditionalists, who know how to write advertising that sells products and services. So, we're at a crossroad. Down one runway are harried *Old School* marketing pilots, who are challenged to use some of the *New Marketing* Internet stuff to prop up traditional methods of advertising. Down the other runway are the *New School* pilots, who need seasoned *Old School* co pilots. Before you buy a ticket, understand it still is not proven that social media can brand products. The phrase *Old School* does not infer that the proponents are not nimble of mind and open to new ideas. The opposite is true! Both pilots, Lindbergh *and* Zuckerberg, are needed.

One of the biggest mistakes you could make is to advertise in the Kitty Hawks' In-Flight Magazine just because your competitors are running ads in it. Don't for a minute think that all your competitors know what they are doing advertising-wise. For example, in rough economic times, many of your competitors will stop advertising. When they pull out of the marketplace, they leave high-profile broadcast "availabilities" for direct-response advertisers to capitalize on. That's the time for direct-response advertisers to benefit from these high-profile opportunities, which are simply not available to them in a strong economy.

The passenger on the airplane who stops advertising to save money is like a man who stops the clock to save time. The passenger's name on the ticket is Fool!

There are many more destinations than just flying on the wings of the social media. Enough with the airplane analogy, the point has been made,

Now let me share some traditional advertising and marketing guidelines with you. Guidelines for who? Guidelines for start-up owners and for small and mid-size-company CEOs who have an advertising agency of record. These check points will give the executive who is responsible for signing off on the agency's creative a reference point for evaluation. It's a mental comfort level. Ad agencies, on occasion, do make mistakes. Here what you should look for:

Placement: Where your advertising appears is every bit as important as what the message contains, maybe even more so. Don't advertise on a left-hand page. This has been tested again and again. When you read a publication, your eyes are drawn to the right-hand page as you flick through, so statistically more people will see your ad if it's on the right-hand page. Leaf through any magazine; the basic layout that has been proven through the years is as follows: you see Photo . . . then the Copy . . . then, at the bottom, the Call-to-Action. The grid leverages our natural tendency to view ads with an S-curve eye motion, sweeping from top left to around the middle, coming to rest at the bottom. There are always exceptions to the rule. Make your ad agency give a sound answer to why the layout?

Visual: Make sure the headline is a killer, a "hook" that will grab the reader or listener. The big question that needs to be asked is "Does it grab you?"

Visual: If the picture is doing the heavy lifting, make sure the *Headline* doesn't flex its muscle.

Subhead: The Subhead is what explains the Headline. For example: The ***Headline*** reads "Who Plays With His Own Balls?" ***Subhead:*** "Tiger Woods uses Nike's new golf balls!"

Body Copy: Research shows that only 12% of the readers read the body copy. Many times you don't need body copy to make your ad work. White space is very powerful. Advertorials are certainly the exception to the rule; they are all body copy.

Testimonials: What others say about you is more powerful than what you say about yourself. It's virtually guaranteed that you'll increase your print response rate by at least 35% by using testimonials. On TV & Radio, you *must* have testimonials and more testimonials.

There are four different types of testimonials:

1. Customers (See commandment # 7)
2. Celebrities (Not always credible because they are being paid)
3. Experts (It doesn't matter to prospects if the expert is being paid)
4. Expert Organizations (Respected organizations carry weight)

Infomercials: Effective communication is a process. Traditional advertising using a single big-idea concept or mere lifestyle messages limits itself. By contrast, infomercials and DRTV commercials persuade consumers by layering a set of core sales messages so that the viewer has more benefits to motivate them to buy. Generally speaking, a commercial has a stronger call-to-action. Again, see Commandment #7, The Six Secrets to Stardom.

Radio: Done right, Radio is a powerful direct-response medium. Radio is a trusted friend. You have a loyal, captive audience. In Radio, you're not buying a commercial; you're buying an audience. One of the first things you want the listener to hear is who you are, so you need to mention the name of your business within the first line or two. The key to success on Radio is frequency-begetting reach, so you must have a budget large enough for every listener to hear your message x number of times. The radio station representative will tell you how much money you'll need to invest to get the needed frequency.

Joy of SFX: A sound effect (SFX) can lead to a concept. Find a sound that has something to do with your product or category. If applicable, weave it into your commercial. Example: AAMCO's two horn blasts.

Negotiate: Never pay the full rate for advertising. Most advertising rate cards are far too high and you can always negotiate. If you're a small business, remember that large companies who use ad agencies are buying based on the readership or audience levels rather than the rate card—so haggle and negotiate. If you can pay 20% or 30% less for your advertising, it can sometimes turn an unprofitable ad campaign into a successful one. No matter what medium you choose to run in, advertising is a numbers game. You want to spend as little as possible, as effectively as possible, to reach as many people as possible in order to make the phone and your cash register ring.

Conclusion:

Stormy weather is forecasted for the Kitty-Hawk's flight plan. Today, the web allows you to fly higher over the retail storms. The pilots of the twentieth-century focused on controlling the customer's mindset. The twenty-first-century manager must let the customer define quality and market acceptance. Now, profitability is more important than sales volume. In today's economy the names of your internet passengers must be Affiliates and Alliances. Otherwise, you won't get to your destination. Plane's name is "SkyAds."

23rd Commandment:
Thou Shall Skip Purgatory

Purgatory is a waiting place where you either go up or down. You don't have to be Catholic to know that when your sales are stagnant, you're in a business purgatory. It's a very precarious place to be. Either your sales are going to go up or you're going to be going to a very hot place.

Fifty years of helping companies get free passes out of purgatory affirms in my mind that sales stagnation always lies in the company's present sales approach. Advertising and lowering prices are not the stimuli you need. You need your sales force to resemble the Energized Bunny on steroids. I guarantee that you won't accomplish any goal you set if you yell, coerce and exert more quota pressure. I recommend that you take a new tack, one that is *"Knowledge based."* It's not enough to say our customers are our number one priority! You need to commit to knowing all about the companies or clients you are servicing.

The 1st Key is Education. The sales people will have to invest their time to educate themselves about the businesses of the potential clients you're going to pitch. With the internet just a *mouse click* away, they really have no excuse for not being informed. It's your responsibility to invest the time to make sure that they are prepared before making their *KC* calls or attending meetings.

My number one secret to impress a potential client and gain his/her confidence instantly is my *"Get Smart"* TV approach. Prior to scheduling the presentation meeting, I conduct (for my edification and education) a cursory Focus Group. I want to find out if the dogs like the customer's dog food. The Focus Group usually consists of eleven people who would be reflective of the buyer's customer base. They evaluate the customer's collateral materials, website and our recommendations. The key is to make it *Maxwell Smart* simple.

What do you do with the findings? Aha! At the meeting and after the opening preliminaries, I inform the prospect that I have conducted a very simple Focus Group so that I would be well-prepared for our meeting. "May I have several minutes to share the findings with you?" 99% of the time the buyer or investor will smile and say: "Please do, I'm interested." At that moment you are in power because you have his interest. Perceived knowledge is power! You have chocolate-coated the vegetable so what he wants will be. You're on your way to leading the prospect down the path to a buying commitment.

Caveats: If the group you're presenting to are investment bankers and venture capitalists, go back to the 10th Commandment and refresh your mind as to what to say or not to say, to get your way. If the product is technical and requires participants who have specific industry knowledge, then the *Get Smart* approach would be too involved and expensive to conduct. If it's at all possible conduct and present the survey. Your goal is: when a person looks up the word *knowledgeable*, they will see your picture.

The 2nd Key is Find the Real Reason. The second key for increasing sales is to use the *Russian Doll* approach to unpeel the real reason why a person needs to buy your product or service. When travelers go to Russia, one of the souvenirs many people bring home is a *Russian Doll*. The uniqueness of the doll is when you remove one doll layer, another doll appears beneath it. When you peel back that doll, again another appears. Usually, there are five hand-crafted dolls within each Russian Doll. This analogy is very appropriate as it illustrates that the deeper you dig, the more knowledgeable you will become. Knowledge closes sales.

The 3rd Key is Investigation. To me, a sales person is a good detective. Train each sales person to be like TV's *Lieutenant Columbo*. Ask questions, take notes and listen intently to the customer's spoken words and to their body language. Taking mental notes is vital. *Columbo* doesn't rush to get every word of vital importance spoken, nor should you. He listens and lets the sales situation evolve. He does a wonderful job of adjusting his questioning to fit every situation. Columbo never presumes to be the smartest detective in the world. He is humble and always reminds his suspects how accommodating they are to let him impose on their busy schedules. These are opportunities to compliment your potential customer.

The real sales pros pretty much know the answers to the questions they are asking. (This is where the *Law of Predictability* (found in the

1st Commandment applies). I recommend that, in this Investigating stage, you mix data-gathering questions with situational questions. For example, if you are selling home-security devices you can ask: "Wouldn't you feel more confident about entering your home knowing you would be warned beforehand if there was any danger that could befall you?" What does that question do? It raises a prickle of alarm on the back of your prospect's neck about the possible danger of walking into an unprotected home. Creating that emotional involvement is a requirement in any selling situation. Train your sales force to be story-tellers.

The 4th Key is the Enthusiastic Handling of Objections. The Handling of Objections is where I differ from traditional Sales Managers. Successful sellers concentrate on Objection Prevention, not on Objection Handling. Objection Prevention is another derivative of the *Law of Predictability*. Want to close the sale? Then mentally walk in the buyer's shoes. Determine ahead of time what you would ask if you were the buyer. Before he/she can ask it, present it as an Implication Question.

Typical examples would be: "I'm well aware of the ROI concern you have for the media dollars spent." Then paraphrase your answer to the question you proposed. "How will this problem affect your future profitability?" Then answer your own question. "What effect does this reject rate have on customer satisfaction?"

The 5th Key is the "Getting to Know You Phase." The opening questions still fall into two categories: "*Getting to Know You*" and "*Permission to Ask*" questions. This is the "sniffing-out" process. The length of time for the preliminaries varies greatly. In the rural South, many times the "getting to know you phase" is 75% of the discussion. Questions like: "Where do you come from? Do we have mutual friends? Did your uncle keep horses?" Whereas, in the garment district of New York, there's a good probability that there will be no chairs in the buyer's office for you to sit down. There might even be a sign on the wall behind the buyer's desk that reads "Spit it out and get out!" Typically, the California market is very laid back. They may offer you Evian water, but that doesn't mean they want to know you right now. They want to see a demonstration. They want systematized bells and whistles. If they like what they've seen or what has been demonstrated, now you can drink the Evian and socialize. If not, the Evian bottle leaves with you, unopened.

Behavioral research shows that many women buyers become suspicious of people who begin by raising areas of personal interest. They feel that the seller's motives aren't genuine and that's an attempt to manipulate them. Chocolate-coded vegetables are not the preferred dessert.

The 6ᵗʰ Key is Tell, Show and then Sell. The sales force needs to be storytellers and showmen. The Y generation doesn't like to be sold, but they like hearing a story or watching a demonstration. Great salespeople are great storytellers. (Revisit the 5th Commandment. Thou Shall Become a Storyteller). I want to stress again that storytellers never keep turning around and read what's on their power-point screen. That's just proving you have a keen eye for the obvious. Pros let the power-point punctuate their story

The 7ᵗʰ Key is the Close. The last step is the asking of closing questions that lead to a buying commitment. The third red flag is not knowing how to close the sale. Too many times I have heard entrepreneurs talk themselves out of the sale. In many cases, all you have to do to close the sale is ask for the order, then shut up! You have nothing to lose by asking a prospect for a decision. If you have shown how your product or service will help them, have confidence in asking for the order. In this area, unfortunately, the classic closing techniques taught in most sales training programs are ineffective and may be abrasive to a major buyer. Beware the closing techniques that can be effective in smaller accounts may be detrimental when used with large companies.

Conclusion:

Several years ago I was in the office of a prominent CEO who was so rushed and harried that he turned to his assistant and said, "I'm under the gun. I don't have the time to buy my daughter a birthday gift. Buy her something girlie!" In a tornado exit he was gone, leaving his assistant with a dumbfounded look. She never had the time to ask him how old his daughter was or what her interests were, what she would like or how much he wanted to spend. It's quite obvious that if you don't have knowledge you can't perform. **Though seemingly absurd, that dilemma occurs way too often when a salesperson calls prospects without knowing what gift that person wishes to hear. In all cases the gift is what you can do for them.** You can't deliver unless you do research before the call. I would recommend social engineering to gain the intelligence needed. Although time-consuming, the *Knowledge Approach* will be the octane that will drive your sales.

The "*Knowledge Approach*" is in tandem with appointment-setting skills. Once you get the prospect on the phone don't say the following:

* We are the most capable in your Industry. *P*rospect: "According to what criteria and how does that affect me?"
* We're the most respected. Prospect: "Oh, really, by whom?"
* We are committed to quality. Prospect: "That's nice, who isn't?"
* I just want 30 minutes of your time. Prospect "Why should I? It can't be that important if it can be told in 30 minutes."

Here is an example of an appointment-setting presentation that eliminates the no-nos.

Mr. Prospect, (*first name if possible*), I'm _____ with _____. I understand that your company is in the process of (*Fill in with your acquired smart intelligence*). Is that correct? (*Wait for a response*). What are you hoping to attain? We can help you because we have experience with similar situations. I read in (name trade journal, newspaper etc.) that you have (Fill in your acquired knowledge). I'm in a position to provide you a solution to your challenge (sell the pain). What's your schedule like next (pick a date) so we can discuss this opportunity in more detail? What time is best for you (morning or afternoon? I'm looking forward to our meeting (Repeat time and date). See you then!

The *Knowledge Approach* is really power in disguise. It's a free card to get out of a sales purgatory. "There is no knowledge that is not power." Ralph Waldo Emerson.

24th Commandment:
Thou Shall Not Steal A Sunbeam

An entrepreneur's hopes and dreams are woven of sunbeams. Beware, a shadow annihilates them. If you're an entrepreneur, do not be around negative people. Over the years we have heard that advice time and time again, but there was never any real proof that negative associations can be so harmful. Now there is!

John Gottman's pioneering research on marriage suggests there is a "magic ratio" of five-to-one in terms of our balance of positive to negative interactions. Gottman found that marriages are significantly more likely to succeed when the couple's interactions are near that five positive remarks/feeling to a one ratio of negative comments. When the ratio approaches one-to-one, marriages "cascade to divorce." Gottman proved that to be so.

In a fascinating study, Gottman teamed up with two mathematicians to test this model. Starting in 1992, they recruited 700 couples who had just received their marriage licenses. For each couple, the researchers videotaped a 15-minute conversation between husband and wife and counted the number of positive and negative interactions. Then, based on the five-to-one ratio, they predicted whether each couple would stay together or divorce.

Ten years later, Gottman and his colleagues followed up with each couple to determine the accuracy of their original predictions. The results were stunning. They had predicted divorce with 94% accuracy, based on scoring the couples' interactions for 15 minutes.

Words make us laugh and cry. They can wound or heal. They can encourage a new business idea or kill it! If you're a confident entrepreneur with a great concept or a small business owner wanting to launch a new product, protect your hearing; build a mental fence around the idea to keep the naysayers' words out.

Sunbeam-stealing and parade-raining . . . these are very serious violations to the human condition. Nothing is more crushing than harboring a treasured dream, an entrepreneurial idea, only to share it with someone and have them say in an off-handed manner: "Nah, that'll never work, pass the ketchup."

Caution: many times the harshest critic is your spouse. The reason? Most times, an out-of-the-box-thinker marries a more conservative thinker. Before you hear how it may not work, find a business optimist who will treat your idea as a true treasure. To me, an optimist is a 90-year-old man who gets married and looks for a house near a school.

I'm not down on pessimists. If there weren't any, I wouldn't feel so good when I accomplish my quests. I'm open-minded; if optimists have their day in the sun, so should pessimists. Of course, pessimists would worry about sunburn.

There is nothing more fragile than a business idea. It comes from heaven unassembled. While it's being assembled you need to be cloaked with optimism and positive affirmations. Why is that so important? Because every business pioneer and inventor has had to weather a daily storm of, "*that's a crazy idea!*" It goes with the territory. When the idea is told, it sounds so grandiose (Man will fly), so far-fetched (I'm going to connect everyone in the world and become a billionaire), so revolutionary (I'm going to invent a horseless carriage) that only the strong-willed succeed. Unfortunately, too many times an out-of-the-box-thinker stifles his idea rather than be thought a fool by sharing the madness. Every ones needs affirmation to keep their dream alive.

Select a person who will keep a secret. Blabbers around a water cooler have a tendency to drink an entrepreneur's idea dry. Woe be to you, the dreamer, if the person you choose is a blabber. It may cause you to lose time, face, funding, patents, investments and more.

A Dream is shared with you!

If someone takes the risk of sharing their dreamscape with you, you must immediately know that you are walking on hallowed ground. When one does open up the jewel box and let you see what is inside, that is a privilege. Dream-sharing is a very, very sacred act. When someone does share their secret hopes with you, the cardinal commandment is: "Thou Shall Not Steal a Sunbeam." Put another way, it is "Thou Shall Not Rain on Someone Else's Parade." My axiom: If you can't be encouraging, then at least be vague.

Chances are, the dreamer has considered sharing his dream with you for a long time. This will not be a random act. To him, you seem like the kind of person who can be encouraging and trustworthy. So here, in a nutshell, are the responsibilities of those who have been chosen for the precious task of dream-sharing. First and foremost, be able to keep a secret. Blabbers don't get the privilege of hearing the private recesses of another person's soul. If you can't keep a Tupperware seal on another person's dreams, you should decline the opportunity.

Once you have someone else's secret inside you, it is critical that you *ziplock* it until the dreamer asks you to take it out for discussion. First of all, even if you have some very critical things to say, first congratulate him. Tell him all the good things he wants to hear about the idea. Once you have established sincere appreciation, then you may begin by asking pointed questions like: "Have you considered doing it this way? Are you averse to considering this strategy?" Let the *well-thought-out-series of questions* communicate your critical comments. It is okay to launch into an extremely tough conversation. It is expected of you. That is one reason you were chosen for the task of dream-sharing. Chances are, now that you are in the dream loop, your advice will be sought again and again until the dream reaches fruition or dies.

The most important thing to remember in all of this is that helping somebody paint their sunbeams is not a paid position. Your interest, encouragement and good advice will be offered gratis to the universe. Don't expect anything. What you'll get is warm fuzzies in your own karma pile and that is very, very good. Someday you'll have a great and wonderful idea and, when you do, someone will be there for you too!

Building Self-Confidence

I have a wonderful exercise for you to do. It's guaranteed to turbo-charge your self-confidence. Doubt is dissipated when you are confident. If you doubt yourself, then indeed you will not seize the opportunity. It's hard to fight a battle when your enemy has outposts in your mind.

The exercise has three components: **Research, Articulation** and **Posting**. You begin by researching for quotes that you find inspiring. You'll need to find three quotes for each of these four categories: #1. Drowning Out the Dream-Crushers, #2. Being Persistent, #3. Being Persevering, #4. Being a Positive Thinker. Researching is an integral part of the exercise. You'll be training your mind to look for positive affirmations. Once programmed, your mind becomes a Geiger-Counter for detecting positive-thinking quotes. Once you have chosen your nine motivational insights, say them aloud and hear how they sound. The final step is to print them out and immediately post them where you can see them on a daily basis. Sometime each day say them aloud. Continue to seek other motivational quotes. There are many websites where you can type in what kind of quotes you are looking for.

To start you off, here are my twelve (12) inspirational quotes:

Drowning out the Dream-Crushers
#1. "Pay no attention to what the critics say. A statue has never been erected in honor of a critic." Jean Sibelius

#2. "Our doubts are traitors and make us lose the good we oft might win by fearing to attempt." William Shakespeare

#3. "Keep away from people who try to belittle your ambitions. Small people do that, but the really great will make you feel that you, too, can become great!' Seek them only." Mark Twain

Being Persistent
#1. "Don't find a fault; find a remedy. Persistency is what will drive you to finding a remedy." Henry Ford.

#2. "Persistency backed by horse-sense makes for success. The key word is horse-sense." Dale Carnegie

#3. "A great deal of talent is lost to the world for want of a little courage. Every day sends to their graves obscure men whose timidity prevented them from making a first effort." Sydney Smith

Perseverance
#1. "Even the two snails got on the ark!"

#2. "When the world says 'give-up', Hope will whisper "try it again!"

#3. "Winners don't Quit and Quitters never win!"

Importance of Positive Thinking
#1. "What we think, we become." Buddha "We are what we repeatedly do." Aristotle
#2. "If you really put a small value upon yourself, rest assured that the world will not raise the price. We earn our income at the same level we think at. Then think Big!" Author Unknown
#3. "It's not the mountain, but ourselves that stand in the way of the climb." Edmund Hillary

You will find that as you discover more meaningful quotes, you'll want to write your own. Here are a few of mine that were derived from doing the exercise above:

* Success comes in *cans*, not in *can'ts*. I *can* do it!
* Life's problems wouldn't be called *hurdles* if there wasn't a way to get over them.
* The road to success is dotted with many tempting parking spaces. Why stop? It's only a little bit further.
* *"I can't"* isn't a reason to give up. It's a reason to try harder.

Sleepless Nights weren't mentioned in the Business Plan
Where was it written that you were not going to spend quite a few sleepless nights staring at the ceiling, worrying about the business or the new venture? Unfortunately, it goes with the territory. I certainly have been awakened with a rush of anxiety. When I come to the end of my rope, I tie a knot and go read my Bible. Here's a verse that you will find comforting: Philippians 4:4 (Paraphrased) *The Lord said Rejoice! Do not be anxious about anything. If you believe in Me, I'll give you a peace beyond understanding".*

When you wake in a cold sweat, you have a choice to worry or worship, to panic or pray. If you worship, the Lord promises to give you peace. Ronald Reagan said it best, "We are never defeated unless we give up on God."

It's essential that you wind down before you go to bed; it is essential for your well-being. No listening to TV's negative news before bedtime. Go to bed with happy thoughts. It's better than a sleeping pill! During the day you need to realize that your days' activities reflect your sleep or lack of it. Invite positive people to be part of your day.

Guess Who's Coming to Dinner Exercise

You know the old conversation starter: If you could throw the ultimate dinner party for 4, which 3 famous, *living* people would you invite? I couldn't decide on just three guests, so I broke my dinner parties up into six themes. This exercise is to give you a valuable insight into what interests you and what type of people you want to have around you. Way too often we are around people or subjects that don't interest us. It wastes time and doesn't advance your business. It's of paramount importance that you never invite a negative person to your dining table. They are not **ever** invited! This may sound cruel, but I would never take a homeless person out to lunch for business advice. How can he help? He doesn't even have a mailing address.

I have set forth below seven dinner parties, each having its own theme. There are two columns. The one on the left is filled-in with my invitees. The column on the right is blank and it's there that you insert your guests' names. This is not a right or wrong exercise. It will give you a clear picture of the type people you enjoy and could learn from. This exercise tees up the *Rushing the Business Community Fraternity* exercise.

DINNER INVITATIONS

My Guest List	*Your Guest List*
Imagine the table talk!	**Imagine the table talk**
Simon Cowell, TV Producer	_____
Mel Gibson, Actor/Director	_____
William Shatner, Actor	_____
Laughter	**Laughter**
Steve Martin, Comedy Genius	_____
Ellen DeGeneres, Television Host	_____
Terry Fator, Ventriloquist Extraordinaire	_____

Sports	*Sports*
Tiger Woods, Golfer, Former #1	_____
John McEnroe, Tennis Announcer	_____
Shaq O'Neil, Basketball Player	_____

Spiritual—Motivational	*Spiritual—Motivational*
Rick Warren, Author "Purpose Driven Life"	_____
Dennis Pragger, Radio Host	_____
John Hagee, Pastor-Evangelical	_____

Explosive Politics	*Explosive Politics*
Rush Limbaugh, Radio Host	_____
Nancy Pelosi, Speaker of the House	_____
Newt Gingrich, Professor—Former Speaker of the House	_____

Business—Science	*Business—Science*
Donald Trump R.E. Billionaire	_____
Martha Stewart	_____
Mark Zuckerberg Facebook Guru	_____

The following exercise expands on Commandment # 10 :

One of the OPMs in raising money was *Other People's Might*, the concept of getting to know and socialize with the kingpins in a person's business community who could be a major help to them. It's like rushing a fraternity. The drill below is designed to help you identify the *Mighty One*, who can help you to fund or make introductions for you. I'm not talking about your friends; it's about making new contacts with the *Mighty One*.

You're Going to "Rush" the So-called Business Fraternity:

What *Mighty One* could you call and ask for financial advice?
_____.

Who could you call to set an appt. with to evaluate the project?
_____.

Who could you invite to lunch that would make proper introductions for you to meet a few elite members of the inner investor circle?
(Business Owners, Bankers, CPAs, Politicians, Country Clubs, Sales Executives)

_____.

Is there anyone in the elite group who has similar interests?
(Golf, Tennis, Fishing, Skiing, Gardening, Church, etc.)

_____.

Conclusion:

Take action and get rid of the toxins in your life that prevents you from being the best.

Replace them with positive-thinking activities and positive people. Even if you're on the right track, the train will run you over if you just sit there. Step 1: Begin today, practice listening to yourself. Think about the negative things you say to yourself. Write them down, no matter how outrageous it seems. Step 2: Analyze if your conversation is punctuated with negative statements. Remember John Gottman's pioneering research on marriages: if every second sentence is negative, they will be divorced in 3-to-5 years. The same holds true for a person's business. It will probably fail. Step 3: It's easier to interrupt a negative pattern of thoughts if you have a clear goal. So check it out. Is it clear? Does it make you feel good? If it's not clear, you know what to do . . . change it. You may not be able to change someone else, but you can yourself.

In summary, Mahatma Gandhi was quoted as saying, "A man is but the product of his thoughts. What he thinks, he becomes." *YOU are the Brand-of-Choice*, and you must think that way all the time!

25th Commandment:
Thou Shall Travel the Road With the Most Assistance

You want as much assistance as possible when you're growing your business. You don't want to travel the least-traveled road, because that path is not lined with people ready to help and cheer you on. You're out there by yourself and you're the only person talking. There are no *low-hanging fruits*.

To grow your sales, all you have to do is first look to the clients you have already sold. These clients are what we call your *low-hanging fruit*. They're ripe and ready to be picked. Visualize a tree with delicious fruit hanging from the branches. Would you struggle and climb to the top of the tree, or would you easily pick the fruit hanging from the lowest branches? Of course you would pick *low-hanging fruit* because it's ripe, ready, and easy to pull off the branch. It's the same with a client. They're ready and open to doing more business with you. You don't have to work so hard. You've already proven yourself by delivering a quality product or service. They know, like, and trust you. You've established a strong client relationship because they can count on you. You now have the opportunity to introduce them to other products and services you offer.

Now that you've identified that your current clients are your *low hanging fruit*, here's a 6-step formula to follow that will help you increase your business with them:

1. Ask for a meeting to give them something.
2. Ask for feedback on your product or service.
3. Ask for referral business.
4. Keep the client updated with what you're doing.

5. Inform them of trends and new technology as this shows you're thinking of ways to help.
6. Stay in touch. Establish a business relationship.

New technology can beget low-hanging fruit. What I mean by that is every day there is new technology that can create new customers for you. You must always be searching for those door-openers. In my case, where I'm involved in producing direct-response TV commercials, Google TV Ads has opened up a new customer base: it's clients with small media budgets who wanted to test television. Google TV Ads is an online marketplace that makes it easy for anyone to buy, sell and measure national TV advertising. Using the familiar AdWords interface, advertisers can easily launch and manage nationally-targeted TV campaigns in the US. Google TV Ads gives you complete control over your TV buy: no contracts, commitments or minimum spend is required.

Through the Google TV Ads platform, advertisers can build campaigns and air ads across more than 98 cable networks. Choose from their inventory to build a customized campaign to reach your audience. Google TV Ads offers national targeting through our partnerships with Dish Network, Bloomberg Television, CBS College Sports, GSN, and other partners.

Using advanced targeting tools, advertisers can find the specific networks and programs that reach the right audience. Google TV Ads' advanced targeting capabilities enables advertisers to have complete flexibility in building a precise schedule that reaches the ideal audience.

With Google TV Ads, you only pay for an impression when a viewer watches your commercial for more than five seconds. This information is gathered from about five million Dish Network set top boxes, so you can be sure you only pay for what you get. Just like with Google AdWords, Google TV Ads utilizes an auction-based pricing system, so you are guaranteed the lowest clearing price in their system for an ad spot.

Innovative concepts can create low-hanging fruit. The key word is "*Innovative*." Think outside the box. Here are some ideas that hopefully will trigger your imaginative mind and come up your own innovative concept that will produce "low-hanging fruit."

1. **Create a Sales Brochure to distribute to your Competition**. It may seem strange to try and advertise to your competition, but you may have a service or inventory they may be able to use. When you visit your competition down the street and you see he has a limited number of bike styles, it's a great time to propose the innovative idea of helping each other. For example, if a customer comes into his shop looking for a particular bike and the owner doesn't keep it in stock, it usually means a lost sale. To prevent that from happening, you guarantee that you will supply him with specific bikes when needed. You then become the "middle-man" for the shop owner. It's a win/win.

2. **E-Zines can also grow *low-hanging fruit*.** E-Zines are online magazines. Their big advantage over print magazines is that they are online. Therefore, everyone who sees your ad has the ability to visit your site. This cannot be said for print magazines. Some E-Zines are directed at a very focused audience. If you have a product that is related to that readership, E-Zines offer an interesting option. When considering whether to place an ad or not, remember that because the reader is online when your ad is seen, that reader can become *low-hanging fruit* with a few mouse clicks,.

3. **Write an "Expert Column" (pro-bono) for an E-zine or for the *local* newspaper or business journal**. It will make you an authority overnight. Remember, in your column provide news and general information of interest; do not, and I stress *do not*, attempt to sell your product; just sell yourself, the *brand of choice.*

4. **Send a simple Postcard**. Here's what you need to do to get started: 1. Acquire a mailing list that is reflective of your potential. 2. Buy a supply of small, inexpensive first-class postcards you can buy right from the post office. 3. An answering service that will let you record a message at least two minutes in length. Because you have chosen the road with the most assistance, I'll share some examples of what to write with you.

NEW PLASTIC SURGERY TECHNIQUE
MAKES YOU LOOK YEARS YOUNGER!
Amazing recorded message gives you exciting
details. Only $2.00 Call (949) 967-Face

HOW TO BUY FORECLOSURES
AT ROCK-BOTTOM PRICES
Call anytime (000) 000-0000 to hear how!

DID YOU KNOW THAT THE BEST MEXICAN
RESTURANT HAS THE LOWEST PRICES?
If you want to know more by listening to a *Free*
recorded message, Call anytime (000) 000-0000.

The next step is to record your free message and mail the postcards. Then sit back and wait for the flood of *low-hanging fruit*. It works, no matter what the business is! Here are some of the reasons why:

(a) You are offering Free information about something the prospect is interested in.
(b) You have taken the "threat" out of making the call when the prospect learns it's a recorded message. The prospect doesn't have to worry if they're going to have to talk to a high-pressure salesperson.
(c) When the prospect listens to your recording, hears what he/she wanted to find out, you have delivered on your promise and become a trusted person.

5. I had figured out how to get people to pay to hear my sales pitch. Although my idea was revolutionary for the times, I made certain I traveled the road with the most assistance. It's foolhardy to think, for one moment, that you can launch a new concept or product without assistance. Don't do it alone.

My idea stemmed from men willing to dial a 900 number and pay to hear a woman passionately profess how much she wanted his body. It was obvious to me if you were to take that concept and apply it to marketing information or a product, you would have a big winner. Imagine, having prospects willing to pay to be sold or to donate.

Here is how it works: You acquire a special 900 number from the telephone company. Once in hand, you run ads or mail letters or somehow entice people to call a 976 number to hear a recorded message of interest. The prospect (one who is dialing the number) must pay the normal charges. Furthermore, he must also pay a fee (usually about $2) for the privilege of listening to information on the 900 recorded messages.

What happens to the $2 fee? The fee is collected by the telephone company. It is added to the caller's phone bill and Ma Bell keeps about $.50 of the fee and sends the rest (about $1.50) back to you. A good deal!

Imagine, if only 3,500 responded, you would have made $5,000. But the real money is in the conversion from caller to customer. If 18% bought, that's 630 new customers times a gross profit of $20 and that's $13,000.

By now you have found out that I never recommend a strategy that I haven't tried and tested. So, let me tell you how I successfully used this money-making concept. The City-Of-Hope, a world-renowned Cancer Center, was contemplating the launch of a major telethon fund raiser. I went to them and said, "As you know, a major cost of airing a telethon is the telephone cost for the 800 number. I have a way to eliminate the telephone expense and eliminate collection expenses." I went to Ma Bell and convinced them to bill the donation to the caller's phone bill, thereby eliminating the collection expense. Because the donator called the 976 number, the 800 number telephone expense was also eliminated. (See commandment #7 to understand the importance of the celebrity roles).

Conclusion:

The use of the 976 concept is a great way to produce *low-hanging fruit* prospects. So, too, are the postcard lead-generators and the other ideas I suggested. But, what drives all campaigns is innovation. A recent survey of CEOs by the American Management Association indicated that 81% considered that *innovation* will be the single most important factor to assure the future success of their business. Innovation will be the engine that drives the corporate ship into the future (*Blue Oceans*).

Some have said, 'innovate or die;" others, 'innovate or evaporate." Whatever the mantra, you know the long-term viability of your company depends on your continuing ability to innovate. You want to have the most innovative people assist you. If you have wilted down your employee search to four candidates, I would recommend you hire that candidate who is most innovative. The word *innovation* is spelled TEAMWORK. The future is going to demand more effective ways of dealing with vendors' innovative ways to improve quality and productivity. No one person is innovative enough to travel the least-traveled road alone. Steve Jobs said it best, "Innovation distinguishes a leader from a follower!"

26th Commandment:
Thou Shall Not Let the Shoe Dictate the Size of the Foot

Analogy-wise, the "Shoe" represents all the people who cramp your God-given talents.

The "Foot" represents the indomitable human spirit. We must not allow other people's limited perceptions to define us. Henry Ford said, "If I had asked people what they wanted, they would have said faster horses."

When we were young we had herculean aspirations. I'm going to be president. I'm going to be a movie star! I'm going to be a doctor. I'm going to be an astronaut and circle the earth. As the years go by, people with many good intentions are too willing to tell you: "You can't do that; you don't have the stamina, musical skills or the intellect." Those people wear "Dream Breaker" shoes. An entrepreneur or a small business owner can't listen to those "cramping" comments.

Listen to your gut. At the height of Jaclyn Smith's career she signed a deal with Kmart. She did so against the advice of everyone she knew. Her agent said it would hurt her acting career. Friends said a Charlie's Angel isn't a Kmart shopper. She was also being pressured by the executives of Max Factor, for whom she was modeling. Kmart made it very clear that they didn't want their spokesperson to lower her glamorous image. The attraction for Jaclyn was that she wouldn't only be endorsing a product; she would be helping the average woman to have an affordable designer wardrobe. In the past 25 years, more than 100 million women have purchased clothing and accessories from the Jaclyn Smith Collection. Sometimes you have to trust your gut. Here's a gut-wrenching exercise I encourage you to take. Write down one big change your gut is telling you to make and then write down the three action steps you can take to make it happen.

We are not limited by our abilities, but by our vision. In fifty business years, I never met a successful business person or athlete who wasn't deaf to those restrictions.

Doctors and scientists said breaking the four-minute mile was impossible. One would die in the attempt. Roger Bannister, the first man to break the barrier, collapsed after he crossed the finish line. The fans gasped with fear that the doctors were right. When he regained his feet, the crowd roared. Bannister acknowledged the cheering with a smile and said, 'They were wrong. I wasn't dead. I never listened. I just imaged that I could do it." If you image yourself as a successful business person, you will be! Without imagination we can go nowhere. Albert Einstein said it best: "Imagination is more important than knowledge for knowledge is limited to all we now know and understand, while imagination embraces the entire world." Imagination explores the world of the unknown. It has no fences or walls.

Man is limited only by his imagination but so few give *Purpose* to their imagination. That's why there are 10,000 fiddlers to one composer. I believe that *Purpose* is the baton that directs imagination. It's the octane that turns dreams into reality. Great minds have purpose, others have wishes.

Without inspiration in the equation, nothing great ever gets accomplished. One person with a belief is equal to a force of 99 who have only an interest. The true and only key to success is having the inspiration to continue to *persist*. The difference between people who are successful and who are not is *purpose*. Have *purpose*, not wishes. Don't wish for what you want, Don't wait for what you want. In the best-seller book, The Purpose Driven Life, its author Rick Warren writes *"Be paprika-hot about what you want out of life."*

In my case, I'm passionate about mentoring young executives. To that end, I wrote this book to be a mentoring guideline! Now that I'm on the back nine of my life, I'm purpose-driven more than ever. I've learned that life is like a roll of toilet paper. The closer it gets to the end, the faster it goes. My advice, no matter your age, is don't count the days; make the days count! Don't wait; begin today imaging the success you will achieve.

For years I have heard people complain to the Lord, why haven't you let me hit the mega-million dollar lottery? God's answer is simple: "*You didn't buy a lottery ticket.*" That answer also applies to being successful in business. You have to buy a ticket and get started.

Free Video "Seeing is Believing"

Because I passionately believe in the power of visualization, I have produced a video to cover topics that are best understood when seen. Yours to download. Go to www.FawcettMarketingWizard.com

Reading this book and understanding the 26 Commandments just saved you $60,000 in MBA tuition.

Step-Up and I will meet you at the top.

www.ingramcontent.com/pod-product-compliance
Lightning Source LLC
Chambersburg PA
CBHW031959170526
45157CB00002B/470